CONVERSION NARRATIVES IN CONTEXT:

Muslims Turning to Christ in post-Soviet Central Asia

by

Daniel Gene Hoskins

submitted in accordance with the requirements

for the degree of

DOCTOR OF LITERATURE AND PHILOSOPHY

in the subject

RELIGIOUS STUDIES

at the

UNIVERSITY OF SOUTH AFRICA

Supervisor: Prof GJA Lubbe

JUNE 2014

© 2016 EMS Press
All rights reserved. No part of this work may be reproduced or transmitted in any form or by any means, electronics or mechanical, including photocopying and recording, without the prior permission of the publisher. The only exceptions are brief quotations in printed reviews.

Published by EMS Press
5511 SE Hawthorne Blvd., Portland, OR 97215
www.emsweb.org

Conversion Narratives in Context:
Muslims Turning to Christ in post-Soviet Central Asia
By Daniel Gene Hoskins

ISBN: 978-1945607004

ABSTRACT & KEY WORDS

Religious experience is a narrative reality, while it certainly relates to doctrines and rituals, it is embodied by the stories people tell which express the meaning of conversion as understood by the converts themselves. In order to enter this narrative world we must engage the actual stories told by converts, making space for their narratives as they make meaning of their experiences and thus open windows on the emic perspective. Sometimes this happens through stories that are largely thematic—expressing conversion in mainly one metaphor. Other times, narratives may touch on many different ideas, allowing us to discern various internal structures, such as some of the factors leading to conversion.

Nevertheless, as important as these narratives are, they are only part of the picture because religious conversion always takes place in context. Therefore, if we are to properly understand the deeply personal experience we call conversion, we must frame it within the social, cultural and historical currents swirling around that experience. The conversions in this study are rooted in the religious history of Central Asia, particularly the seventy-odd years of Soviet rule. By the end of that era, it is probably more appropriate to think in terms of localized *islam*, rather than a universal religion based on the text of the Quran. Not only so, but the once proudly distinct Muslim peoples, now living under Russian rule, had become enculturated into Russian patterns of life, thought, and worldview, a process referred to as *Russification*, something which had profound effects on the way some of them have experienced conversion away from their natal religion.

This study examines both of these aspects, first the contextual and then the personal, through the stories of thirty-six Muslims who converted to faith in Christ in post-Soviet Central Asia. By exploring the deeply personal and the broadly contextual together, this study offers a clear view of the meaning of religious conversion, in a historical, social, and religious context.

Key Words:

Central Asia, post-Soviet, *Russification*, religious conversion, Narrative Inquiry, Islam, context, Grounded Theory, qualitative research, Social Constructivism,

ACKNOWLEDGMENTS

To my dearest wife Linda. Your love and encouragement has helped me become much more than I would have ever been on my own. In every way, you share in this accomplishment.

Table of Contents

1. Introduction 1
    1.1 Conversion 2
    1.2 Context 4
        1.2.1 Geographic Context 5
        1.2.2 Religious Historical Context 7
        1.2.3 Cultural Context 16
    1.3 *Russification* 19
    1.4 Problem Statement 25
    1.5 Statement of Purpose and Research Question 26
    1.6 Research Approach 27
    1.7 The Researcher 28
    1.8 Assumptions 32
    1.9 Rationale and Significance 33
2. Literature Review 37
    2.1 Literature Related to Religious Conversion in General 37
        2.2.1 Philosophical 38
        2.2.2 Sociological 46
        2.2.3 Anthropological 53
    2.2 Literature Related to Muslim Conversions to Christianity ... 62
    2.3 Literature Related to the Context of Islam in post-Soviet Central Asia .. 70
    2.4 Located this Research Vis-à-vis the Literature 78
3. Methodology 80

 3.1 Theoretical Paradigm 81

 3.2 Qualitative Research Approach 83

  3.2.1 Analytical Approaches 83

  3.2.2 Research Sample 89

  3.2.3 Data Collection Methods 95

  3.2.4 Data Analysis Methods 99

 3.3 Ethical Considerations 102

 3.4 Reliability and Validity 104

 3.5 Limitations of Study 106

 3.6 Summary of Methodology 107

4. Findings and Analysis Related to *Russification* 110

 4.1 A More Grounded Picture of *Russification* 110

 4.2 Metaphysical Location of Jesus/*Isa* 116

 4.3 A Textual Faith 125

 4.4 Agency 132

  4.4.1 Russian Agency 137

  4.4.2 Agency by Muslim Background Converts 141

5. Findings and Analysis – Miscellaneous 148

 5.1 Conversion as Spiritual Migration 148

  5.1.1 Push Factors 149

  5.1.2 Pull Factors 156

 5.2 The Three Languages of Conversion 167

  5.2.1 Language of Joining 168

  5.2.2 Language of Rejecting 174

      5.2.3 Language of Believing 178

  5.3 Conversion as non-Linear Movement 186

6. Conclusions 193

  6.1 The Research Question Revisited 193

  6.2 Contributions 197

  6.3 Directions for Further Research 199

  6.4 Personal Reflections 200

Bibliography 201

Maps

Map of Central Asia 6

Tables

Table of study participants 92

Chapter 1- Introduction

This study will investigate the conversion narratives of Muslims in post-Soviet Central Asia who have converted to Christ. This is a qualitative research project which also places a major emphasis on the context in which these conversions are taking place. The qualitative aspect of the research will use Grounded Theory and Narrative Inquiry as the analytical framework[1]. The aspect of the thesis that explores contextual matters is rooted in Social Constructivism which posits that phenomena can only be properly understood in their context. This points us toward the title.

Taken together, the title and subtitle of my thesis do their job without being too fancy; they frame the topic, describe the content, and give structure to how that content will be explored. Also, you will note that I chose to subsume the topics and content into the subtitle so the title proper would be focused on theoretical framing. Thus the first two words of the title point to two very significant abstractions—conversion and context[2]—that will give us access to the meanings I want to explore in this thesis. That said, the most logical way to begin is to delve into each of these concepts as a means of setting the groundwork for the rest of the thesis; first we will look at conversion, and then at the various dimensions of the study's context.

---

[1] A detailed explanation of Grounded Theory and Narrative Inquiry, and why I have chosen to use them, is found in chapter 3, Methodology.
[2] Obviously this leaves out a key term in the title, "narratives." However, since issues related to the use of narratives is primarily a methodological concern, I will reserve that discussion until chapter three, Methodology.

1.1 Conversion

As long as there have been organized religions, people have, for various reasons, shifted allegiances from one deity to another, or in the parlance of narrative studies, between different supernatural metanarratives. Sometimes this shift is total and complete, a dramatic break like the quintessential Christian conversion story of the Apostle Paul[3], the narrative that Christian theologians and scholars have traditionally considered typical, even normative, of Christian conversion (Segal, 1990; Kim, 2008). For others, the experience of conversion is better described as a long process of rewriting their personal narrative, more of a revision of a story rather than a completely new one. Modern scholarship widely recognizes this complexity; consequently many models have been proposed to understand it (Buckser & Glazer 2003; Hefner 1993; Rambo 1993; Stark & Finke 2000). Due to this complexity, any formal definition of conversion is problematic at best. Nevertheless, in order for a word to be useful, it must have some degree of shared meaning between writer and audience, so I will begin by constructing the parts of a working definition, and then move on to related constructs.

Many attempts have been made to succinctly describe the complexity of religious conversion in the century or so since scholars first reflected on it apart from theology proper,[4] three of which most resonate with me. The earliest of these is from Arthur Nock, who called conversion "a deliberate turning from indifference or from an earlier form of piety to another, a turning that implies a consciousness that a great change is involved, that the old is wrong and the

---

[3] The conversion of the apostle Paul is found in Acts chapter nine, and retold by him in chapters twenty-two and twenty-six.
[4] See chapter two, Literature Review.

new is right" (1933, p. 7). A much newer and even more concise definition that I find quite insightful comes from anthropologist Diane Austin-Broos who said that conversion was "a form of passage, a turning from and to, that is neither syncretism nor absolute breach (2003, p.1). And finally, Roger Lohamann offers a slightly non-conformist definition that resonates with my research when Lohamann suggests that religious conversion is best understood as "taking on a relationship with new supernatural beings" (2003, p. 117).

There are several reasons why I have chosen to use these three definitions for framing the term conversion, but primarily it is because they hint at important elements which will emerge over the course of this paper. Specifically it is these points that resonate with my research; Nock's "turning from indifference or other form of piety," and "consciousness that a great change is involved;" Austin-Broos' "turning from and to[5]" and "neither syncretism nor absolute breech;" and Lohamann's "relationship with new supernatural beings." Despite deficiencies in each of these three[6], I am content for them to loosely work together as somewhat of a working definition. Nevertheless, given that my thesis is rooted in a Grounded Theory approach to data[7], further consideration of the meaning of conversion will be saved until chapter four, Findings and Analysis when I will explore the meanings that emerge from the interviews.

However, there is one philosophical concern that I should address before moving on. Some scholars have contested the very use of *conversion* in regard to the religious experiences of non-Western peoples. For example, philosopher Karl Morrison contends that conversion should

---

[5] The phrase "a turning from and to" was originally used by Rodney Stark (1993, pp. 2-3).
[6] If taken individually, each of these definitions has problems; Nock is overly influenced by the theology of his day, leaving no room for continuity between old and new, Austin-Broos is too vague and lacks *religious* substance in her definition, and Lohamann's quote is within in a context that is condescending toward people of faith.
[7] The implications of using Grounded Theory will be dealt with in chapter three on methodology.

not be used as an instrument of critical analysis because it is not appropriate to all cultures and religions (1992). I concede there is a measure of truth in this claim, but I believe it is overstated, particularly in this case. This thesis will examine religious movement across severely contested lines, between Islam and Christianity, religions with a long history of enmity between them. Thus it is hard to imagine a better word to describe movement between these camps. Furthermore, I find Saudi Arabian born anthropologist Talal Asad's position on the matter more convincing than Morrison. Asad states that while Westerners from Christian societies may at times confuse concepts when using the term *conversion* in non-western contexts, it is still a valid term to help approach "the narratives by which people [have] apprehended and described a radical change in the significance of their lives" (1996 p. 266). With that said, we can move on to the matter of context.

1.2 Context

After trying to understand the nebulous concept we call conversion, it might seem that defining "post-Soviet Central Asia" would be easy, but *au contraire*, the region and its peoples are somewhat of an enigma. Or in the words of my friend Dr. Morgan Liu, Central Asia is "the most curiously over-determined yet understudied region of the world… [at the] confluence of the far more scrutinized Middle East, China, Russia, and South Asia" (2011, p.2). This dearth of knowledge presents us with a problem and I would argue that understanding this context is immensely important to understanding the conversion narratives I have gathered. Therefore I will explore the context of these conversions, Muslims living in post-Soviet Central Asia, at some depth and within a framework of three interlocking concerns—geographic, religious history, and cultural.

1.2.1 Geographic Context

This is the easiest of the three to deal with because geography is the most concrete aspect of context I will address, and from this perspective, "post-Soviet Central Asia" is relatively easy to delimit. The region is sometimes referred to as the five CARs, the states of Kazakhstan, Kyrgyzstan, Tajikistan, Turkmenistan, and Uzbekistan, each of which gained their independence at the break-up of the Soviet Union in December of 1991. This research will focus on former Muslims living in only three of these countries—Kazakhstan, Kyrgyzstan, and Uzbekistan (see map on next page).

Map 1: Central Asia (Nations Online Project 2013)

Secondly, physical geography plays an important, sometimes neglected role in human affairs, and in this case, the fact that these three countries have contiguous territories plays an important role in how to delimit my study population. The Pamir Mountains to the South of this troika and the Qyzylqum Desert to the West, cutting Uzbekistan in half, have long been formidable boundaries to significant, sustained interaction between cultures. Thus people in these three countries have had more interaction, thus greater commonality with each other, more than they have with those of the other Central Asian republics.

So, by limiting my study population in this way, I was able to gain a wide sample, across ethnic lines, while avoiding the complications which might arise by drawing study participants from the entirety of Central Asia. If, for example, I had included participants from Tajikistan in the study, I would have been faced with integrating their slightly different historical context as Persian peoples and Shia Muslims[8], into the analysis. This creates a fitting transition point for discussing the historical aspect that frames this study.

1.2.2 Religious Historical Context

The history of Central Asia is fascinating since it is filled with empires, wars and the famous Silk Road which for centuries was the only link between China and the rest of the world. However, it is not the *general* sweep of history that is our concern in this thesis. Since it concerns the context of the conversions studied in this thesis, it is the *religious* history of Central Asia that is important—vitally important. I would like to briefly return to an earlier quote from Diane Austin-Broos that conversion was "a turning from and to" (2003, p.1). It seems to me that most conversion studies so emphasize the experience of turning itself, and the religious system which a person turns *to* that they tend to forget there is also something they have turned *from*. Therefore, although I will attempt to limit the scope of this section as best I can, I must give it some space to unfold because the issue of *"turning from"* can cover quite a bit of breadth.

Before the arrival of Islam, the regions of our focus were known as Bactria and Soghdia. The religious milieu was a mixture of Zoroastrianism, Christianity, Buddhism, and indigenous forms of animism. And while Islam arrived early, with the Arab armies in the mid-eight century,

---

[8] More on this below in sections on Religious Historical Context, and Cultural Context.

it remained primarily the religion of the ruling classes through the Umayyad and, Abbasid Caliphates (Moffett 2009). Even with these early Muslim overlords, the older Christian communities remained important elements of the religious landscape. This is evidenced by the fact that some cities thought of today as centers of Islamic civilization, such as Samarqand and Bukhara, were, during the early Islamic era, "metropolitians" of the Syriatic Church, implying large numbers of Christians existed in and around these cities (Latourette 2003, p.323).

Then, in the early thirteenth century, the scourge of the earth arrived in the region—the Mongol armies led by Genghis Khan. The slaughter and destruction inflicted in the region by his horde became proverbial. The Arab historian Ibn al-Athir called it a "tremendous disaster such as had never happened before, and which struck the whole world, though the Muslims above all. If anyone were to say that at no time since the creation of man by the great God had the world experienced anything like it, he would only be telling the truth" (cited in Spuler 1972, p. 30).

Much more could be said, but to the point, while the damage inflicted by the Mongol armies was brutal, it was quite temporary. Within less than one hundred years the great Mongol empire was crumbling in Central Asia and soon the Turkic successors to the Khan converted to Islam, thus causing it to regain status as the religion of the ruling elites (Khalid 2007). In the late fourteenth century Timur, a Turkic prince who used marriage to tap into the enormous charisma resident in Genghisid line, began to establish a new empire centered in what is today the Ferghanna valley of Uzbekistan. His efforts would create a new high point in Islamic culture and eventually Central Asia would become a new center of Islamic civilization. A contemporary, Mirza Qazvini, described Bukhara, the second city of Timur's empire, as comparable to the very seat of the Caliphate, Baghdad, "adorned with the brightness of the light of doctors and jurists," and "embellished with the rarest of high attainments" (cited in Juvaini 1958).

During this period of Islamic resurgence it appears that the only other significant religious community in the region was the Christians. And although they were in in decline, they still had a visible public role. This is evidenced by the fact that Nestorian Christians were able to operate a training college for clergy in Central Asia, in the Turko-Mongolian language, at least as late as 1340 (Dickens 2001, p. 16). However, eventually the Timurid rulers brought the long Christian presence in the region to an end and the region became, thoroughly and completely Islamic. It is also believed that it was on account of the Timurid rulers that the name *Turkistan* came to be used for the region. Specifically, the part of Central Asia pertinent to this thesis was called *West Turkistan* to differentiate it from the portion of the Turkic homelands that were intermittently under Chinese overlords—*East Turkistan*. Thus, despite the rise and fall of small kingdoms in some of the oasis cities, *West Turkistan* is the name by which the region would be known even after Soviet authorities began carving it up into ethnically-linked administrative areas (Adler 1946).

After its zenith during the Timurid dynasty, Islam in Central Asia began a slow process of calcification. The reasons are many, but two interrelated points stand out. One, because of the generous grants to mosques, madrasas[9], and Sufi hospices during the Timurid era, the *waqf*[10] in

---

[9] In Modern usage, a madrasa is an institution of higher learning where the Islamic sciences are taught, as opposed to and elementary school of the ordinary type (Pedersen 1986, p. 1123).

[10] The *waqf* was a tax-free property endowment that could be established for pious benefit or public utility. Some examples of the beneficiaries of *waqfs* are mosques, schools and graveyards (pious); or bridges, poor houses, and public drinking fountains (public). The key determining factor in those established for public benefit was that the

Central Asia became a powerful and wealthy institution. This caused a systematic impulse to protect the existing power structures by limiting access to the original textual sources of authority, the Quran and the Hadiths. And next, over time as fewer and fewer individuals had access to these sources of authority, other collectively held cultural artifacts became Islamic identity markers. In other words, ancestors, holidays, and lifecycle events slowly took the place of knowledge and adherence to Islamic doctrines (Khalid 2007). As decades turned to centuries, Islam in Central Asia became a collection of folkways and life-cycle rituals for the majority of the people, rather than a set of doctrines and practices (R'oi 1995, p. 83). The result was that even prior to the Soviet era, Central Asian Islam had become a meta-ethnic construction, similar to the designation *Turkic*.

A fascinating insight into this worldview and construction of the meaning of Islam comes from an official history written for the Khan of Khwarazim[11] in the early nineteenth century. This massive volume begins with the biblical Adam and then leads to Noah's grandson named Turk—the progenitor of all Turkic peoples—and from there through their collective national history. In this account the Turkic peoples appear to have always been Muslims; it makes no mention of Arabia or the arrival of Islam in Central Asia (Munis and Agahi c. 1928). What is remarkable is that not even the Prophet Muhammad appears in this version of Islamic history! Islam is presented as if it were virtually synonymous with what it means to be Turkic. Thus, for the

---

beneficiaries were all Muslims or that the Muslim population of a given area collectively have the right to use the utility (Peters 2002, p.60).
[11] Khwarazim was first the name of an administrative region under the Abbasid Caliphate, but by this time was only a small oasis kingdom, located on what is today to border between Uzbekistan and Kazakhstan.

majority of Central Asians, Islam had become "*islam*"[12] (spelled without the capital), or perhaps "local Islam." The religion brought to the region by Arabs had become subsumed into local identity and changed into just another part of the Turkic genealogical heritage. The importance of this cannot be overstated because it demonstrates that Islam as a civilizational force and universalizing religion was already in full-scale retreat before the arrival of the Russians and later the Bolsheviks.

Into this retreating Islam entered the Russians soon-to-be-Soviets who, soon after solidifying their political control began a massive attack against religious structures and sacred spaces. The institution of *waqf* was ended and all their properties confiscated, mosques, madrasas, and shrines were destroyed or closed. The official Muslim Spiritual Administration for Kazakhstan and Central Asia was established which gave the government a significant level of control over the few mosques, madrasas and clerics which were allowed to remain (Hiro 1994 & Louw 2007). The result of this limited access to physical sacred spaces was the further weakening of the root of Islamic knowledge and the "long-term transformation of religious culture" (Khalid 2007, p. 82).

It is worth noting that the "transformation of religious culture" which Khalid notes was not isolated to the Muslims who came under Russian/Soviet rule. After the collapse of the Ottoman Empire, there was a discernible trend toward the secularization of life in many Muslim lands (Ro'i 1995). However, since in Central Asia this process was driven by outsiders, i.e. the Russians, the secularization of life was much more contested by Muslim communities. Open

---

[12] Abdul el-Zein has made a strong case that there are many "islams" observable if one approaches Islam anthropologically rather than essentially (1977).

resistance such as the nationalist *Bashmachi* (meaning "bandit" in Uzbek) in the early 1920s (Hiro, 1995) are not of concern here, but more passive forms of resistance are since they have an impact on the way Islam developed in the region through the Soviet era. This passive resistance to Soviet ideology seems to have taken two distinctly different paths, both of which have their roots in Central Asia's pre-Russian past.

The first group who passively contested the Soviet's campaign against Islam were those who became known as the *Qadmichilar*, or traditionalists (Murphy 1992, p. 191). These Muslims maintained their identity primarily by clinging to their cultural practices, which they reinterpreted as being Islamic. For example, Polakov notes that *kalym*, or the brideprice traditionally practiced by all Central Asian cultures, was considered to be an essential feature of Islam (1992, p. 55). But since the Soviet state was actively promoting ethnic identity as a necessary evil, cultural expressions of Islam were not treated as threats to state power.[13]

The second source of this passive resistance was known locally as *Jadidchilar*, or reformers (Murphy 1992, p. 191). The *Jadid* movement wanted to modernize Central Asian Islam, to free it from its backward ethnically oriented stagnation (Ro'i 1995). What Muslims called reform, or *Jadid,* Soviet authorities dubbed "parallel Islam" included any and all activities of Soviet Muslims which took place beyond the control of the Soviet Spiritual Directorates. This unauthorized version of the faith was propagated by a slowly developed network of itinerate clerics and unauthorized, underground mosques and simple prayer rooms. At its most basic, this was little more than small groups in homes conducting prayers, but in some places it included all

---

[13] See section below on Cultural Context.

the religious services a devout Muslim family might need though the cycles of life (Myer 2012, p. 187). "Parallel Islam" seems to have come to the attention of Soviet authorities first in the 1960s (Ro'i 1995), but became a major concern at the time of the Khomeini revolution in Iran (Wimbash 1986, p. 227-228). There is significant evidence that extensive underground Islamic societies existed even after several decades of government repression. In the mid-1980s, a study by the Soviet Academy of Social Sciences found "comparatively extensive practice of [Islamic] traditions, festivals and rites among all socio-demographic groups of population" (Ro'i 1995, pp. 13-14). Yet in testimony to the impact of the anti-religious purges, that same study also found that these unofficial Islamic "religious leaders had little or no religious training," and that they "clearly based their leadership role on folk practices" (*ibid* p. 15).

By now it is obvious that the generally accepted view that Islam was decimated by the militant Atheism of the Soviet Union is not completely accurate. Certainly the Soviet state exerted enormous pressure on the Muslim community, but due to what had already happened, I believe Khalid's description of a community transformed is more accurate. Other than a destruction of physical sacred spaces, this pressure primarily acted to accelerate existing trends. Specifically, this refers to the migration of religious identity away from scriptural sources and toward ethnic ones, causing religion to become even more of a "local *islam*." In other words, while Muslims in Central Asia will always continue to share certain normative features with their coreligionists in other areas of the world, directly before, during, and after the Soviet era, the term Muslim is best understood in Central Asia as a meta-ethnic identity, similar to the designation "Turkic" (Khalid 2007).

With this in mind I find it fascinating that some social scientists are already writing about the "Russian-Soviet parenthesis" in Central Asia (Laurelle, 2005, 41). In other words, some view the combined Russian-Soviet impact on Central Asia as little more than a parenthesis in a sentence, important because it somewhat interrupts the larger flow, but not critical to meaning.

This also points toward the status of Islam in Central Asia since the collapse of control from Moscow in 1991. It is my contention that for understanding conversions in the region, there is no need to specifically assess Islam in the post-Soviet era in order to understand the religious context of my research. Yes there has been a proliferation of mosque building in the post-Soviet era, and indeed more people are publically participating in Islamic ritual, but that nicely sums up the degree to which things have changed because at the level of practice, the majority of the Muslim population fits the profile I have previously painted.

A survey done in 2011-2012 by the Pew forum for Religion in Public Life serves as a nice illustration of this point. It showed that for most Central Asians, Islam is still more an aspect of their ethnic identity rather than a religious practice. As it concerns Muslims in the three states connected to this study, Kazakhstan, Kyrgyzstan, and Uzbekistan, below are some of the results that are representative of their level of religious practice:

- On average, how often to you attend the mosque for *Salat* and *Jumah* Prayer[14]?
    64% answered seldom or never

- Outside of attending religious services, how often do you pray?
    58% answered seldom or never

---

[14] *Salat* refers to the five-times-a-day, daily prayers, and *Jumah* are Friday prayers.

- Do you fast during the holy month of Ramadan?

    84% answered NO

- How often do you read or listen to the Quran?

    56% answered a few times a year or never

Or in the words of one visiting Turkish scholar, in post-Soviet Central Asia "there are Islamic sentiments and feelings, but they lack true knowledge" (Kimmage 2005).

But that raises important questions such as, "What *is* the meaning of all this religious history?" And "What does 'being a Muslim' mean to a person whose worldview has been shaped by the religio-historical context above?" To begin, we must lay a bit of groundwork because even the term "Muslim" has a wide spectrum of thought associated with it. On one end of the scale is the essentialist view made famous by Edward Said, "Islam does not develop, and neither do Muslims; they merely are" (1979; p. 317). If this static view of Islam, so common in religious studies, is combined with essential Islam's orthopraxy, then a Muslim is preeminently someone who practices the fundamentals of the religion of Islam (Denny 1993). On the other end of the scale would be the classical anthropological approach of someone like Clifford Geertz who would tell us that a Muslim is someone whose "systems of significance—beliefs, rites, meaningful objects" (1968, p. 95) has been shaped by Islamic thought.

By this time it should be clear that I thoroughly disagree with the essentialist view since it presents Islam as some kind of decontextualized global monolith. On the other hand, while I lean toward the anthropological view, given the historical context I have detailed above, that too is not a perfect fit. The classical view of anthropology is that there are core symbols in all religions which are the building blocks, in this case, of an Islamic worldview (Ortner 1984, p. 130). But as we have seen, over a very long period of time the universal Islamic "core symbols" were overtaken by cultural symbols that are not necessarily rooted in essential Islam, and community belonging as markers of one's identity as a Muslim. By the end of the Soviet era, for vast majority of the indigenous population in Central Asia, being a Muslim had very little to do with classic Islam, it meant being part of a community that saw itself as Muslim, not individual knowledge of sacred material or regular practice of Islamic rituals. Therefore, for the purposes of this thesis, a Muslim is anyone who understands himself as part of the Muslim community, or in the case of converts, anyone who claims to have been part of such a community in the past. This means my use of the term "Muslim" will be a self-designation, anyone who described themselves as a "former Muslim" or "Muslim convert" will be referred to as such.

1.2.3 Cultural Context

The third and final aspect of context that I wish to explore is the cultural one. For the majority of research done in post-Soviet Central Asia, the cultural issue has been framed by ethnicity, yet I have deliberately chosen to cut across ethnic categories. There are two main reasons for this. First, it seems to me that some of our research objectivity has been hijacked by a *priori* decision about the contours of ethnicity in the region, one that is rooted in Soviet era policy.

It may sound strange to some that the Soviet Union operated with a "positive discrimination" policy toward minorities (Martin 2001), but many aspects of state ideology were negotiated based on ethnic identity. This positive discrimination was developed through an elaborate discourse within the various Soviet academies of sciences concerning "ethnogenesis," that is how peoples came into being with a shared identity. Linguists were instructed to construct distinct 'literary languages' for these peoples so that the political leadership could highlight the differences between peoples who previously had more in common than what distinguished them from each other. Historians painted the picture of specific peoples existing through many centuries, more or less unchanged on the same land. Once these identities became accepted by the political system, they were propagated both by the state publishing system and by hiring decisions within the newly minted republics. As it specifically concerns Central Asia, the end result was that despite the many imprecisions of Soviet ethnography, an eponymous people became wedded to a territory (Laruelle 2008) and produced what are commonly referred to as the "titular nationalities" of the region, i.e. the Kazakh, Kyrgyz, Uzbek, etc., those ethnic groups that gained Soviet Republican status. The ensuing decades of SSR status[15] gave the impression that the region was already organized in something similar to the Westphalian nation-state model. Thus at the collapse of the Soviet Union it seemed a rather "natural" transition for the international community to recognize the independence of these ethnically–derived states.

Yet it is easy to forget that these seemingly primordial ethnicities *cum* titular nationalities are rooted in dubious Soviet-constructed ethnic historiographies which were constructed as part of a Soviet effort to create national identities that would undermine the pan-Turkic and pan-Islamic ideas (Shnirelman 2010). As recently as the 1930s there were only three recognized 'indigenous nationalities" Uzbeks, Kirghiz (sic) and Turkmen (Atkin 1992). Not only this, but a large study in the 1970s showed that ethnic identity was fluid in the Soviet Union, particularly

---

[15] SSR – Soviet Socialist Republic.

with people shifting toward titular nationalities such as Bashkirs becoming Tatars and Uyghurs becoming Uzbeks and Kazakhs (Anderson and Silver 1983). Concerning this fluidity, one Uyghur businessman explained to me:

> In the past, Uyghurs lived with the Uzbeks in the Ferghana Valley and they all lived like one people…Then, when Stalin started to have conflict with the Chinese, he tried to divide the Uyghurs as separate, as immigrants from China. When people were standing in bread lines, the official would ask 'are you Uyghur or Uzbek?' If the person answered "Uzbek" they got three or four loaves of bread. If they answered "Uyghur" they got only one. Soon people learned it was better to be Uzbek, not Uyghur, although they had never really thought about the difference before (Kyrgizmanov, S. 2005).

However, on this point I wish to be clear. I am not arguing that the national identities which are usually part of ethnographic research design in Central Asia lack historical grounding. My point is that ethnicity has long been fluid in Central Asia, and as such it is a weak foundation for research design. And because of this weakness, the tendency in Central Asian studies to frame almost all phenomenon, including religious conversion, along ethnic lines has probably caused important insights to be missed, insights that I hope to capture by specifically *not* using ethnicity as either a category of data collection or analysis.

Now, as a means of transition, I would very briefly touch back on the concern that Soviet authorities had with larger, or "pan-" identities because this quite ironically brings us to the second reason I feel we must move beyond ethnicity in our study of conversion in the region *Russification*.

1.3 *Russification*

One of the reasons that ethnic identity has been such a focal lens for studies in Central Asia is that it is located on the opposite end of the spectrum from the discredited "new Soviet man" dogma. In the luxury of hindsight, some scholars have dismissed this major goal of Soviet policy as an ideological fantasy (Kaganovsky, 2004). This dismissal seems to be corroborated because "the new Soviet man," in the sense of a political animal, has now splintered into many different republics. Yet this is another place where we must be careful lest we allow the geopolitical to overshadow our thinking about Central Asia. For even if there is no political entity attached to "the new Soviet man," there is most certainly a meta-identity in the region that shares some of its contours, that is the commonly used term—*russified* Muslims. Usually *Russification* refers to the process of linguistic and cultural assimilation that many non-Russians experienced in the Soviet Union (Bennigsen 1969). In order to properly understand what a *russified* identity is and why it is important in a study of conversion, we should look briefly at both the linguistic and cultural assimilation that are involved.

To begin, we must remember that while "enforced" might be too strong of a word, linguistic assimilation in the Soviet Union was not a strictly voluntary process. The use of Russian by non-Russian peoples was encouraged with specific social, economic, and political aims in mind. First, Soviet authorities theorized that language was the actual location of ethnic consciousness, thus linguistic assimilation would lead to deep ethnic changes (Kholmogorow 1970, cited in Silver 1974). Also, the Communist party (CPSU) promoted Russian proficiency as the "inter-ethnic bond which could hold a Soviet multi-ethnic society together" (Matusziewicz,

2010, p. 213). However, in order to understand the effects of linguistic assimilation, Silver points out that it is useful to distinguish the two functions of language in a setting where there is contact between ethnic groups; a vehicle of communication and a symbol of identity. When language is acting as a vehicle of interethnic communication it becomes a conduit whereby the *other* moves closer, a function that relates to cultural assimilation which I will examine shortly. Silver's second function of language is as a symbol of ethnic or cultural identity—one belongs when one can speak the language. Thus a Central Asian who became bilingual with Russian could not only communicate with Russians, but they would quite naturally feel at ease in social settings that their mono-lingual coreligionists would not (Silver 1974). Over time, this very practical outcome of bilingualism would cause an identity shift, especially in an imperial context where the authorities were actively promoting a new vision of the ideal man.

The other aspect of *Russification* that we should examine is cultural assimilation. This is perhaps best understood by means of two common life experiences in the Soviet era, post-secondary education and Soviet military service. Although some argue for one or the other being the more powerful influence, I see no reason to separate them here because they seem to have very similar contours in the way the affected identity formation of Central Asians. Both required a young Muslim to leave their natal home and live/work/study in a mixed-ethnic setting. Both required the rapid development of Russian proficiency. And finally, both forced them to eat in common dining halls where they would unwittingly abandon Islamic dietary regulations (Khalid 2007 & Benningsen and Lemercier-Quelquejay 1967). Considering the importance most Muslims have historically placed on dietary regulations, and the emotional value of food, and the issues of ritual purity involved, it would seem to me that this last factor would have the deepest impact of the three on a Muslim's sense of identity. This is more a topic for psychological research, therefore I can only speculate here.

I find it quite interesting that the issues raised in the literature are the very things that have come up in conversations with Central Asians about their experiences with Russians. One friend, (not a part of this study) described his service in the Soviet army during the late 1970s. I asked him how it changed him:

> "I was 17 when I went to the Russian army. They sent me far up North into Russia somewhere. I could barely speak any Russian. I was cold and alone. I had to quickly learn to understand and speak Russian to survive because there was no one to translate into Uzbek for me in drill camp. They worked us from early morning until late evening. When they said you could eat, you ran to the dining hall and ate whatever it was they had. I had never eaten pork in my life, but when you are that hungry you don't ask questions about what is in the food.
>
> After two years I came home. Because I now had a skill [welder] and spoke good Russian I got a job at the large pump and pipe factory. At lunch we had a dining hall where all the employees ate. I still did not ask questions about what kind of meat was in food.
>
> So, I have never bought pork to eat, never eaten it at home, but before I really didn't think about it. In those days it didn't matter, food was food" (Sayid A. 2006).

Here we see a snapshot of how theories about the processes of *Russification* look in real life, here is how the culture of one young Muslim man changed. These two things, service in the Soviet military and post-secondary education, were watershed events for countless Central

Asians like my friend above. Uzbeks, Tatars, Kazakhs, Uyghurs, etc. left home as peasants, but returned after a few years as Soviet citizens. Serving, studying, and eating side-by-side with the *other*, Russians, Ukranians, Koreans, etc., helped to forge a different identity.

The combination of linguistic and cultural assimilation produced a common sense of citizenship and shared experiences. However, I contend they did not create a completely shared identity with Russians, something which might be implied by the term "*russified* Muslim." The commonality that many Muslims in the former Soviet Union feel toward Russians must be understood as a genuine coexistence of their Islamic and/or ethnic identities within a new Soviet one (Khalid 2007), not as a complete loss or subsuming of their Islamic identity in the Soviet one. This is because the assimilation factors we have explored, i.e. the power of continued shared cultural space with other Muslims, such as family members, community obligations, as well as other minor ones we have not explored, would not have been enough to fully assimilate a Central Asian into Russian culture. This experience of inhabiting two cultural spaces created a distinctly new cultural identity—a hybrid identity—the *russified* Muslim. And this is why the concept of *Russification* is so important as part of the context of the conversions in this study. But before delving into that, I think it would be expedient to lay some groundwork.

When a person develops a hybrid identity, several things happen. Important to this study is that it allows a person to maintain an identity "homeland" while simultaneously building a social capital in a new identity "location." In this situation, the *russified* Muslim kept a sense of belonging to the Islamic community while building an identity in Soviet social/political/economic space, thus acquiring a means of social mobility. However, it is important that we understand hybridization as more than a pragmatic strategy for personal or family advancement. The bifurcation of identity is also a way of resolving internal-external conflict for peoples living under colonial rule (Werth 2000). Rather than suppressing the tension of cultural ambiguity, this fusing of identity renders the choice between social worlds unnecessary because it *enables* a person to carry markers of both Muslim and Russian identity at the same time, and without any sense of contradiction. People with hybrid identities culturally inhabit "an ambiguous third space… with different cultural identities brought into dialogue with each other" (Barnett 2008, p. 3).

This is precisely where the importance of understanding *Russification* can be seen in this study of conversion. What Barnett calls an "ambiguous third space" I would argue is in fact a new culture, or at the very least a significantly different sub-culture. Because it is a different cultural background it has a huge impact on how people experience religious conversion. In other words, the Uzbeks, Kyrgyz, Kazakhs and others who participated in my study were significantly different from their ethnic coreligionists in Northern Afghanistan or Northwest China, even though they share not only ethnic identity but live in close geographic proximity. Nor are they simply bilingual people who could therefore access information about the Christian religion in the Russian language. But these are people who inhabit an overlapping, yet nonetheless different, cultural space. They are members of a meta-identity that goes beyond both their ethnic and Islamic ones. They are very specifically *russified* Muslims who have converted to Christ.

To bring the matter context to a conclusion, the first major contextual consideration has to do with the religious history of the region. Due to many factors, for the majority of the population in Central Asia, being a Muslim has little to do with classic Islam, it means being part of a community that is Muslim. The identity as a Muslim which most study participants held prior to conversion[16] had very little to do with individual knowledge of sacred texts or the regular practice of Islamic rituals. Or, in the words of an old Muslim friend in Almaty, Kazakhstan who said a Muslim is anyone "one who nursed at a Muslim breast."

Secondly, concerning cultural identity, the indigenous ethnic identities we are familiar with are, to a certain degree, political artifacts and have long been quite fluid. Thus I have argued that we need to move beyond the categories of Kazakhs, Kyrgyz, or Uzbeks in our social analysis. Also, as it concerns cultural context, the impact of *Russification* is such that is has created in a new hybrid identity—a *russified* Muslim. Thus I would contend that we must consider the study participants as members of a distinct culture, or at least a distinct subculture as *russified* Muslims. It follows that analysis of conversion in such a context must differ significantly from studies of people who have left the classical practice of one religion to join another.

Finally, despite my best efforts to thoroughly explicate the context in which this study is immersed, we should keep in mind that no analysis can even begin to mirror the variety and complexity of a real world context (Isichei 1970). The best we can do is consider contextual

---

[16] There were a few participants who were much more observant than the majority, and those cases will be noted and dealt with as needed in chapter four.

factors with all due diligence, all the while remembering that religious conversion will always be, to some extent, a mystery.

1.4 Problem Statement

Since the break-up of the Soviet Union a little more than 20 years ago, significant numbers of Muslims living Central Asia have left their ancestral religion and converted to faith in Christ[17]. Protestant Christian missionaries view these as victories for the global expansion of their faith, while Islamic and political leaders denounce these as subversive, even pseudo-religious financial frauds (Noor 2012). But somewhere beyond the heated rhetoric and inflated egos of those on the periphery of the phenomenon itself, at the core there are people who are making weighty choices about what they believe and with whom they will identify. There has been very little research into these conversions, and none that I can find which was both rooted in the actual narratives of converts and gave serious consideration to the specific socio-religious context. This brings us to the purpose of this study and the research question that will guide it.

---

[17] Typically these conversions fit into the larger theological framework of Protestant Christianity. However, since few of the study participants used that framework as a self-descriptor, I will refrain from doing so until chapter four concerning findings and analysis.

1.5 Statement of Purpose and Research Questions

The purpose of this study is two-fold. One, to learn what the personal narratives of Muslim converts to Christ in a post-Soviet, Central Asian context tell us about emic understandings of conversion. And two, how contextual factors may have influenced the way these conversions are experienced. In order to explore this in the widest possible way, my research has been guided by the following questions:

- What is religious conversion?
- What kind of *islam*[18] are converts turning *from* in Central Asia?
- What is a "*russified* Muslim" and how might this influence subsequent conversion to Christ?
- What can we learn about the meaning of their personal conversion experiences from the content of these narratives[19].
- What insights about the nature of conversion itself can be found in the stories of converts in Central Asia?

Or to state the research idea as one succinct question:

<u>What do the conversion narratives of Muslim converts to Christ in post-Soviet Central Asia tell us about the way they understand their conversion, the contextual influences on their conversions, and the nature of religious conversion itself?</u>

---

[18] The use of lower-case i in "islam" signifies local expressions of the religion as opposed to "Islam" capitalized to denote its universal characteristics and expression.

[19] Content analysis is only one of several different approaches to narrative inquiry. The rational for this choice will be explained in chapter 3, Methodology.

1.6 Research Approach

This investigation represents what could be called a multi-case study of conversions. In-depth interviews were the primary method of field data collection. I began the interview process by conducting two pilot interviews which I used to filter questions and shape the approach to conducting the interviews which I would eventually use. In the end, the information obtained from thirty-six individual interviews formed the basis for the findings of this study. The interviews were conducted in either Russian or English, depending on the choice of the participant. They were taped, recorded, and transcribed verbatim.

This data was later coded using an open codebook, developed according to actual content of the interviews, yet guided by the study's conceptual framework. Finally the data was analyzed in several ways. One, I examined the occurrence of codes across different interviews to weigh possibilities for generalization. Two, commonly occurring codes were operationally defined by interview extracts. Three, the coded material was analyzed in light of the contextual matters laid out in chapter one. Four, theories were developed from the interview data that both explained and illustrated the findings.[20] These four steps were not exactly sequential, although there is a certain logic and flow to the way they are presented above. In practice they would be better described as recursive, that is, they were repeated and overlapped as necessary to best derive meaning from the data.

This approach has helped me avoid a common problem that Daniel Varisco deals with in his book *Islam Obscured*. He argues that much ethnographic writing about Islamic peoples is

---

[20] The specifics of coding, analysis, and theory development are covered in chapter three, Methodology.

filled with *researchers* telling what Muslims say or do, and contain very little of what *Muslims* themselves actually say or do (2005). Thus in the end, this produces new theory that is not so much derived from the participants as it is from the researcher's perceptions of them. My approach has, I believe, produced findings and theories more rooted in the actual words and meaning constructions of study participants than in my observations and ideas.

1.7 The Researcher

Although I have focused on deriving meaning and constructing theory from the words of study participants, it is still true that "the researcher is the instrument in qualitative inquiry" (Patton 2002, p. 566). This does not mean that social science findings are completely subjective and thus not as valid as those obtained with inanimate tools such as microscopes or algorithms. However it does mean that the background and perspective of the social science researcher are likely to exert a more obvious imprint on their findings than in other disciplines. With this in mind, it seems appropriate to describe my own background which led to this particular thesis.

My family and I lived in post-Soviet Central Asia on and off for twelve years, 1997-2009, about half of that time in the country of Kazakhstan and half in Kyrgyzstan. During this time I had a number of different jobs, ranging from community development worker in small NGOs to being an assistant professor at the American University of Central Asia. My interest in cultural studies was kindled soon after we moved to Almaty, Kazakhstan where I found the encounter with non-Western peoples, particularly post-Soviet Muslims, fascinating. Working at a local NGO required me to quickly learn Russian and regularly interact with local people, and due to the nature of that work, most of our interactions were in *their* context not mine. This caused me to develop a keen interest in local culture. Also, early in our sojourn in Almaty, I met Dr. William Clark, a cultural anthropologist who had spent many years in the region. We spent many hours discussing culture, religion, and other topics as my family attempted to become acculturated to the region.

This confluence of factors stirred in me a latent desire to do what I later came to know as participant observation, and so I began doing informal ethnographic interviews as a hobby, writing them up for my own pleasure. Eventually Dr Clark challenged me to formalize my study of Central Asian culture by under taking an M.A. from William Carey International University, in Pasadena CA, where he served as an adjunct instructor and became my academic mentor.

Later my family moved to Kyrgyzstan, where I worked for another NGO, but this time specifically for ethnographic research and related consulting. Through that organization I conducted three ethnographic studies: a two-year project about the long-distance Muslim traders who link NW China and the Ferghanna valley, the next to study the concepts of marriage held by Muslims in Kyrgyzstan, and a short ethnography about how Muslim converts to Christianity view expatriate Christians.

During more than fifteen years of involvement in Central Asia, I have observed, first hand, enormous change in the region. One sphere of change that has held my keen interest is the shifting religious environment. I have watched Islam struggle to resurge among the largely nominal Muslim population, as well as seen a significant number of Muslims who have converted to various forms of Christianity. With great interest I have observed the impact across social, cultural, and political domains as these two religions have jostled for adherents. This eventually developed into a desire to understand these conversions better. This naturally led to my research questions and the topic of my thesis.

As for my current research activities, in addition to this thesis, I am a Senior Research Associate with Fruitful Practice Research. This is a collaborative research team that is studying the "best practices" of Christian NGO workers in various parts of the developing world and then developing training based on those findings. My role involves qualitative research design, field data collection, analysis, and training. Since 2008 I have worked alongside several researchers from different disciplines, and this has had a large and very positive impact on my own development as a researcher.

Finally, to be forthright about possible biases, I should state that I am a devout Evangelical Christian. My family's involvement in Central Asia has always been "missional," that is we have always made decisions around a core value of taking the message of Jesus to the people with whom we live and work. Nevertheless, I have spent many years deliberately trying to develop the academic objectivity and identity, even concerning topics that are of great personal importance. However, in this particular study, it seemed that many people needed to affirm my Christian identity, or categorize me in a way they were comfortable with, before they would participate in the interviews. Kathryn Kraft encountered a similar response in her study of Arab converts:

"Converts would not accept anyone who claimed to be a neutral researcher; if they were to talk to me, I had to be "for" them; otherwise, they would conclude that I was "against" them. This helps to explain why many of them chose to believe that I was more than just an academic researcher" (p.56).

This confirms what Raymond Lee found concerning any research with highly stigmatized populations—that the researcher needs an identity which clearly establishes their *bona fides* as a person with whom participants can interact safely and without reserve (1993, p.67). Therefore, it is fair to say that it would have been impossible to access this particular study population without having a clear Christian identity. On the other hand, it seemed important to some participants that I was conducting truly academic research, not strictly acting as a "missionary." It seems the many participants viewed me as both an insider *and* an outsider to the world of Christian mission. I believe this was due to three factors; one, I have carefully cultivated an academic identity over the years with some of these individuals; two, my formal interviews were conducted some years after I had lived in the region; and three, the way in which I conducted the interviews was specifically designed to project this insider/outsider image.

Finally, I would assert that there is no inherent contradiction to being an evangelical Christian and conducting high quality academic research. Having strong beliefs, even to the extent of sharing them with others, is neither unusual nor exclusively Christian. Over the years I lived in Central Asia I worked with Christians, Muslims, Atheists and Agnostics. Many of these were as committed to their "faith" or worldview as I am to mine. These individuals ranged from an American anthropologist who was a dedicated propagator of the LGBT worldview[21], to devout members of the Muslims Dawa movement, to other Evangelical Christians like myself. Ultimately, the question is not whether an academic can have a personal faith and still do professional research; but whether or not he can maintain objectivity in his work. I take pride in the fact that I have spent years developing the ability to separate my personal feelings from my work, thus I am persuaded my faith does not in any way distort my research findings, but in fact facilitated this research.

1.8 Assumptions

As with all research, there are fundamental presuppositions from which my work flows. Based on my personal background, experiences and academic training, this research will reflect the following basic assumptions. First, although conversion is a distinctly religious issue, it is not the exclusive domain of theology. Moreover, because my aim is to develop emic understandings and grounded theories, I believe the disciplines of Anthropology and Sociology, rather than of Divinity, are better positioned to wrestle with the topic. Secondly, although I have argued that Muslim conversions to Christ in Central Asia are taking place in a fairly unique context, they are still products of a highly interconnected world. Therefore I do not expect the experiences of conversion in this study to be so different as to fall into the classic Orientalist trap of painting them as the *other*. Recognizing the peculiarities of context is different than radicalizing it. And finally, I assume that all the personal stories shared with me are true. I did not cross-check them

---

[21] (LGBT) Lesbian-Gay-Bisexual-Transgender.

nor did I approach them with significant skepticism. This does not mean I consider every fact and detail of each story to be precise, rather I am asserting that none of the study participants were attempting to deceive me or intentionally misrepresenting their experience[22].

1.9 Rationale and Significance

Although the Soviet Union has been dissolved for more than two decades, our social science knowledge of its soft underbelly in Central Asia is still woefully lacking. This lack of depth has often caused the Muslims of the region to be associated with the ongoing turmoil in Afghanistan of Pakistan due to geographic proximity and the appellation -stan. Alternately, and just as incorrectly, despite the fact that Muslim make-up the vast majority of the population in Central Asia, they are often summarily lumped together with Russians because of misperceptions about the Soviet Union. Despite the small measure of truth that exists in all over-generalizations, these both point toward a need for more in-depth social science research in the region.

Another rationale for more diverse social research on the region comes from the over-emphasis that has been placed on one academic discipline, There have been an abundance of books, articles, and studies about the possible geopolitical consequences of these "Muslim" states gaining their independence at the end of the Soviet era. We could spend a great deal of time speculating on why this is so, but the anthropologist Gabriele Rasuly-Paleczek has observed that on the level of the individual researcher, geopolitical studies are in vogue in Central Asia

---

[22] See further discussion in chapter three, Methodology, under the discussion about recollection and fact.

because they mainly rely on quantitative and macro level data, thus do not require long-term field work in a difficult and perhaps politically unstable environment (2005, p.3).

My own experiences in Central Asia reflect this assessment. For example, I distinctly remember meeting a "visiting scholar" at the American University of Central Asia in Bishkek, Kyrgyzstan. He was visiting for three months to conduct research, funded by the US Defence Department, on Kyrgyz propensities toward community violence. As we exchanged research notes, he was quite surprised that I had already lived in Kyrgyzstan for about three years and was planning to spend a couple more "in the field" gathering different ethnographic data. He then leaned over the table in the library and quietly told me he "couldn't imagine living in a hole like this" for so long. I did not find his attitude surprising because not long before this encounter, a friend who teaches in the Central Asian studies department of a major American university told me, "if any research project requires more than few months in the field, it was a very hard sell in this department." With a prevalence of such attitudes, it is no wonder that Central Asian studies suffer from a lack of research produced from the long-term fieldwork of social scientists.

But the dearth of a robust social science knowledge is only one indicator pointing toward the importance of undertaking a new research in Central Asia. Just as important, but concerning a very different domain of knowledge, is the fact that this study will also add to our understanding of conversion to Christ in the Muslim world. Although some research on this phenomenon has been done; Barnett 2008, Greenlee 2005, Kraft 2009, and Radford 2011 to name a few, there are still serious gaps in our knowledge because of the diversity of religious practice and local historical experience across the Islamic world. Furthermore, Radford's study isolates ethnic identity as the primary unit of analysis, something I have already argued against extensively. The nature of Islam in Central Asia was such that for many Muslims their enculturation into Russian/Soviet Culture, or *Russification*, hyphenated their identity, making them participants of a distinct sub-culture.

I will now offer one final rationale for this research. The majority of studies on religious conversion, ones that have produced new theories about conversion, where conducted in the West (I will use the term "West" or "Western" to refer to the United States and much of Europe, as well as other English-speaking countries that are children of the Enlightenment). This means their contexts are liberal social environments where individualistic assumptions about human choices have made a clear imprint on theory development. Clearly this is not the environment of Central Asia where conformity to tradition is of much higher value (Poliakov 1992 & Ro'i 1995). A brief personal anecdote will help illustrate the chasm between the typical Westerner (myself) and a Central Asian.

Several years ago I was trying to learn local proverbs in the Ferghana valley, so I asked a good Muslim friend if he could tell me some that his father or grandfathers taught him. After narrating several, he told one that I did not understand. The words seemed familiar but I could not tie them together with meaning. After several attempts he finally explained it to me and this is basically what he said: "Live your life in the ruts son. Life is best lived in the rut where it is safe." That proverb is the polar opposite of an American cultural maxim I grew-up with, "get out of the rut!" When he told me that this precept had guided his life I had a personal moment of epiphany. Despite spending countless hours developing a close friendship with this man and others like him, I suddenly understood how very great the distance between the worldviews that governed our lives. And it is a graphic reminder that if I want to understand Muslim conversions to Christ in post-Soviet Central Asia, I cannot rely on theories generated in the West, but must attempt to enter their world and draw from that context. And such is what I have done.

Chapter 2 - Literature Review

Overview

It would be hard to overstate the importance of the literature review in the writing of a thesis because "a researcher cannot perform significant research without first understanding the literature in the field" (Boote & Bile, 2005 p. 3). Bloomberg and Volpe contend that the chief purpose of reviewing the literature goes deeper than surveying what has already been written on the topic; rather it is to help the researcher develop a robust knowledge of it (2008 p.47). If my topic were only concerned with one central point, the structure of this review would be quite simple. However, my thesis forms an intersection of different domains of knowledge, and as such requires a more complicated literature review structure. In the hope of at least making this complexity manageable, I will organize my review into three broad fields, religious conversion in general, conversion of Muslims to Christianity in particular, and the *islam* of post-Soviet Central Asia.

2.1 Literature Related to Religious Conversion in General

The literature on religious conversion is wide, and at times feels more like a patchwork quilt than a coherent whole. However, one way that we might bring some structure to this cacophony of thought is to think of it as a continuum. This would range from esoteric works such as William James' classic, *Varieties of Religious Experience*, on the one end, to something like the Hefner's anthropological study, *Conversion to Christianity* (1993), on the other.

philosophical/esoteric   Concrete
●━━━●

Therefore, I will use this simple continuum as a framework to explore the literature on religious conversion, beginning with an exploration of important works in the field of conversion studies that are highly esoteric in nature, then moving left to right toward the more concrete works.

2.2.1 Philosophical

First I would like to consider one of the most abstract books on religion that I have ever encountered, a relatively recent offering, *The Study of Religion in a New Key* by Jeppe Jensen (2003). In all the 454 pages of text, there is not a single example of a living religious experience examined. Despite my own inclination away from this approach to understanding conversion, and that the book is not about conversion *per se*, I found this book had much of value with regards to my study.

For example, although it was surprising in such a highly philosophical work, the author insists that the only thing we really can say about religious experiences is that which is talked about by the participants (pp. 305-306), because religious reality is inherently a narrative construction. Whether it is a Native American shaman passing along his stories to the tribal youth, or the first century Christian evangelists dictating their memoirs of Jesus, the religious world is more narrative than it is tangible. While some would argue that this is true for all of life, this is particularly so for the realm of religion because it does not exist in the physical sphere, but only in a construction of shared reality—and that reality is shared through words (pp. 451-452). This dovetails nicely with the basic premise of Grounded Theory, one of the analytical approaches I will use in this study[23]. Jensen goes on to assert that the only reason that religion is accessible at all is because, at one level, it is a "semantic phenomenon" (*ibid*) i.e. disclosed by words. Therefore, while the spiritual verities that believers profess to experience are beyond the reach of systematic inquiry, because they are shared through words, the analysis of them is not. This is not a trivial point and ties strongly into the other analytical approach I am using, Narrative Inquiry[24].

The author goes on to point out that when we study religious phenomena, we must demarcate between religious beliefs or experiences and the act of systematic analysis. If the researcher does not keep these clearly separated in his mind, he is susceptible to two particular mistakes. He either attempts to apply logic and rationality to "other worldly" entities and experiences, or assumes that understanding religious experience is just as inaccessible as the spiritual "realities" the narratives express. Jensen's cautionary note on this point could help explain why religious studies has taken a "narrative turn" in the past few decades, a trend of which my own thesis is a part. Since religious experience is a shared, semantic experience, then

---

[23] Grounded Theory will be explored in depth in chapter three.
[24] My use of Narrative Inquiry will be explained in chapter three.

it is only logical that the best way to access them is through narratives. So in a strange way, a highly philosophical book like *The Study of Religion in a New Key* has provided extensive support for the concrete, narrative approach I will take in my thesis.

The next book I would consider, *The Varieties of Religious Experience* by William James (1902), is sometimes cited as the starting point of the modern study of religion, as opposed to theology (Alexander, 1980 p. 192). The book is based on series of lectures James gave at the University of Edinburgh and is a regular feature in the literature reviews of many studies on religion and religious experience. As with *The Study of Religion in a New Key,* James is not writing specifically about conversion; nevertheless, he does have quite a bit to say on the subject with two chapters exclusively addressing it.

Despite my placement of this work on the philosophical end of the scale, James does cite the religious experiences of many people, some at length. Nevertheless, his ideas and thoughts seem much more derived from his own personal musing on the topics covered rather than actual analysis of the experiences cited. This is probably due to James' exclusive focus on the psychology of religion, to the neglect of other approaches that help explain religious phenomenon.

Furthermore, James's writings seem strangely contradictory at times. In what eventually becomes a text full of narratives, the author insists in the introduction that abstractions are the best way to understand religious experience (p. 10). However, this contradiction is the book's saving grace. If it were not for James' lengthy citations of actual accounts of personal religious experiences, his work would have been little different from much of the highly theoretical work written before it, and therefore so abstruse as to be almost worthless. In fact, it is perhaps his greatest contribution to the development of the discipline of religious studies in that he helped to shift the focus from the institutional or collective element of religion to the individual and his experience(s) (Nielsen, 1998).

As mentioned earlier, the book contains two chapters on conversion, and these are, in my opinion, perhaps the best part of the book. Among other things, in these chapters, James argues that despite a long Protestant preference for understanding conversion as a dramatic event, there is plenty of reason to believe otherwise. Even in what seem to be examples of instantaneous, dramatic religious conversions, James says it is not a contradiction to view it as a much larger process involving all of a person's faculties (pp. 194-195).

On this subject in particular, James seems to have struggled. Perhaps he was trying to articulate ideas and concepts before their time, before there were sufficient supporting writings in the academic universe to help him properly explore what he began.

As one might expect of any 100-year-old "classic" in its field, there have been many critiques of *Varieties of Religious Experience*, and of James' thinking in general. Only a sampling is possible here. For example, one well-taken criticism from the feminist perspective is that James' work is wholly a "male's eye view" of religious experience full of "Victorian paternalism" (Thistlethwaithe, 1994 pp. 1039-1040). Another, and in my view more substantial, critique is from Toni Morrison (1993 pp. 63 & 120), who observes that not only does James completely ignore African-American religion, but he also uses "dark" or "darkness" metaphorically for the "sick soul" in ways that strongly suggest a racial dimension.

All in all, I was a bit disappointed by James' book. Perhaps it was due to the datedness of the material, or maybe I was disappointed by the heavy emphasis on the psychology of religion, a topic outside my interest. Possibly it was simply due to the under-developed state of the discipline at the time James was writing; the study of religion was just emerging out from under the shadows of Christian theology proper. For whatever reason, I am not alone in my disappointment with *Varieties of Religious Experience*. I believe Dittes summed it up nicely when he wrote about the way posterity has treated James. He is "revered in the first chapter of a textbook, then ignored in the substance of the [same] book" (1973 pp. 328-329).

It is impossible to review the more philosophical end of the spectrum in conversion studies without the spotlight falling on *Understanding Religious Conversion* by Lewis Rambo (1993). Rambo is considered one of the premier thinkers in the realm of conversion and this is largely due to the treatment of the topic in this volume.

One of the first issues that Rambo tackles head-on is the question of voice. When trying to understand a conversion between any two religions, who defines the experience? Do missionaries, whether directly or indirectly involved, have that right, or does the rejected religious establishment? Or do the converts themselves own the right to their experience? Certainly both the etic and emic perspective is of value, but Rambo makes a strong case that the decision *priori,* even before examining the phenomenon, must be "which perspective will direct the research?" Then, he goes on to argue that since "the converts themselves assimilate the faith in the categories relevant to them" (p. 5), the emic perspective is the most compelling of the two.

Not only are Rambo's arguments strong, but also his emphasis is strong support for the methodological choices which I will delineate in chapter 3.

Rambo goes on to propose a holistic model of conversion that offers a framework for exploring a wide range of questions and issues related to conversion. He states that while no model can encompass the entire terrain of conversion, there are at least four essential components: cultural, social, personal, and religious systems, with each carrying a varied weight in each particular conversion (pp. 7-8). He also points out that in the past, scholars from each particular discipline tended to give undue weight to their field's point of view when analyzing conversion. However, since Religious Studies is a holistic human science, relishing insights from several different disciplines, Rambo reminds us all to be more careful in our analysis.

Rambo's holistic model leads us to what he is perhaps best known for, a sequential stage model of conversion. He sees the process spiraling back and forth between the following stages: context, crisis, quest, encounter, interaction, commitment, and consequences. However, rather than exploring the stages in this review, I will focus on the implications of this model—that conversion is more of a process than an event. This is important because Christian theologians and scholars have traditionally considered Paul's sudden and emotional conversion as typical, or even normative, of Christian conversion (Segal, 1990 p. 3) (Kim, 2008 p. 196) (Harran, 1983 pp. 30-31).

For me, one of the most helpful parts of Rambo's work is the chapter on context. The author emphasizes the importance of context in several ways, such as when he writes, "Context is more than a first stage that is passed through, it is the total environment in which conversion transpires" (p. 20). Everything that happens to the convert happens in a particular context or environment. Rambo delineates two kinds of context, macro and micro, the first being elements such as the historical, social, political setting, and the latter being the "more immediate world of a person's family, friends, and ethnic group" (p. 22).

Notwithstanding, Rambo has had his critics. He has been accused of oversimplifying complex issues and having a limited mono-cultural perspective (Blanchard, 1994 p. 738). While I disagree with the first, I must agree with the second. As for oversimplification, from the outset it was clear that Rambo's purpose was to paint an overview of the subject of conversion, not offer an in-depth explanation of all possible theories and concepts. Therefore, we might say that what Blanchard called "over simplification" (*ibid*) would be better seen as conciseness, and in that light, it is a virtue not a vice. However, as regarding Rambo as having a mono-cultural perspective, that is also clear, particularly when he attempts to universalize certain aspects of the human condition which are clearly rooted in a Judeo-Christian worldview, for example, when he observes that a common theme is that conversion results from a sense of guilt (p. 161).

That criticism aside, it would be difficult to over-estimate the importance of Rambo to the study of religious conversion. In my opinion, *Understanding Religious Conversion* towers over other philosophical works in the field because it helps the reader consider many varied aspects of conversion without being overly abstract or obtuse.

Before leaving the more philosophical end of the spectrum, I should at least briefly explain why I will not review works such as the *Primitive Mentality* from Levy-Bruhl (1923), or *The Elementary Forms of Religious Life* by Emile Durkheim (2008, but originally published in

1915), nor anything by Marx. These are certainly important, and highly philosophical, works on religious belief, but I will not include them in my review for two reasons. One, it is difficult to find among these early theorists any serious reflection on *conversion*. They speculated on many aspects of religion—Totemism, witchcraft, and Fetishism to name a few—but conversion was not among them.

However, another reason I have chosen to neglect these works has to do with my philosophical approach to religion in general. Rambo pointed out that, "If we are to be phenomenologically true to the experiences and the phenomena of conversion, we must take the religious sphere seriously… Taking religion seriously does not require belief, but it does imply respect" (1993 p. 11). Yet Levy-Bruhl, Durkheim, and Marx are great examples of doing just the opposite. As Evens-Prichard pointed out, "The persons whose writing has been most influential [on the subject of 'primitive religion'] have been at the time they wrote as agnostics or atheists…Religious belief was to these anthropologists absurd" (1965 p. 15). Today there is growing scholarly consensus on this point. Representative of this is where Bateson et al wrote, "To be blunt, some psychologists [of an earlier era] have tried to conduct smear campaigns against religion in the guise of science" (1993 p. 15). Furthermore, "while it is not necessary that social scientists who want to understand religion be religious, it is necessary that they be able to sufficiently suspend their unbelief so as to gain some sense of the phenomenology of faith and worship" (p. 21). In light of this demonstrated bias, I feel no compulsion to review such theorists, even if they have been historically respected in the field.

2.2.2. Sociological

With that said, I am ready to move to the right of my hypothetical spectrum, away from purely psychological and philosophical studies on conversion.

Philosophical/Esoteric — Concrete

Here, somewhere between the esoteric writing of James or Jensen, and hard-grounded anthropological writings like *The Anthropology of Religious Conversion* by Buckser and Glazier (2003), is where we encounter the more Sociological works on the topic. This is the appropriate place to look at a paradigm shifting article by John Lofland and Rodney Stark, "Becoming a World-Saver: A Theory of Conversion to a Deviant Perspective" which appeared in 1965. This article not only helped launch a new way of thinking about religious conversion, but it also launched the careers of its two authors, both of whom have subsequently written important work on the topic which I will review shortly.

Lofland and Stark studied conversions to a small, millenarian cult that was based on the West Coast of the United States, and this study was instrumental in launching the study of "New Religious Movements" (NRMs) in the United States, something that I unexpectedly found important to my own study[25]. They conducted interviews with several converts and from that data extrapolated new theories about why people convert from one religious worldview to

---

[25] The relationship between NRMs in the US and Muslim conversions to Christ in Central Asia will be explored in chapter four.

another (p. 862). Several of their key findings have significance to my own thesis; these I will very briefly summarize.

First, Lofland and Stark posit that converts must perceive some kind of enduring tension prior to interest in conversion (pp. 864-865). Secondly, Lofland and Stark also point out the importance of what they call "seekership," the active participation of converts in their own conversion. And while, like all the observations in the article, their concept of "seekership" is based on a very Western conversion environment, the active role of the convert has been well-attested to by others in cross-cultural conversions as well (Sanneh, 1989) (Walls, 2008).

Lastly, Lofland and Stark address the issue of "affective bonds," in two directions, bonds within the new convert community, and bonds with those on the outside. The former involves a deep, positive, emotional attraction to others in the group (p. 871), and the latter refers to a lack of affective emotional attachments with those outside the new group (p. 872). The idea of affective bonds seems to be a better, emic way of accounting for Durkheim's analysis of religion as primarily a social construct.

Despite these useful insights, the obvious limitations of Lofland and Stark's work is three-fold; a) the study population was exclusively Western, b) the conversions take place in a pluralistic Western social setting, and c) they converted to a small, minor religious cult. The authors acknowledge this limitation, yet argue that their terms are general enough to function as a starting point for the study of other types of conversion (p. 875). While I found much that is useful in the models put forth by Stark or Finke because of the context of my own study, I can easily imagine settings so vastly different from their research context that their theories would hardly be an appropriate starting place for inquiry. Nevertheless, this article fills an important place in the move toward a more sociological and anthropological understanding of conversion, something both of these writers advance in their future writings.

Moving on to some of the future writings, the name Rodney Stark has become closely associated with the theory of "rational choice" in religion. His earliest attempts to develop it were in *A Theory of Religion* with William Sims Brainbridge (1987). However, he later thoroughly revised and enlarged on these theories in *Acts of Faith: Explaining the Human Side of Religion* written with Roger Finke (2000). This second volume has since become a landmark in the field of conversion studies; therefore, I will review the later.

In *Acts of Faith*, Stark and Finke begin by acknowledging that science cannot access the supernatural side of religion, yet this does not support the reductionist theories, which explain religion as only a projection of society. Since we cannot verify or discredit the supernatural claims of religion, the best thing we can do is to analyze the observable, human side of faith, leaving questions of its veracity to the believers.

And on the topic of religious believers themselves, Stark and Finke devote a significant amount space to making the case that there is no longer any room in the discipline for disrespect towards religious people and what they believe. They clearly demonstrate that many in the earlier generation of theorists, such as Freud, Marx, and Malinowski, did everything within their considerable power to try to label religious people as backward, primitive, ignorant, or even psychologically unbalanced (pp. 3-9). And as I noted previously, Stark and Finke are not the only ones to recognize this.

Stark and Finke's book is organized around a series of propositions about religious faith and definitions of key terms. These are used to explain and expound on several different domains of religions behavior, individual conversion, group religious dynamics, even the relationships between religions and the societies in which they are embedded. In a work such as this, it is hard to isolate which theories or propositions are key. However I will attempt to focus my review on the following three: assigning religious reasons for religious behaviors, rational choice theory, and the theory of religious economies.

First, in *Acts of Faith,* the authors argue that religious behaviors have primarily religious causes. Despite both being sociologists, Stark and Finke reprimand their colleagues for constantly trying to uncover the "real" reasons for religious phenomena, reasons that are invariably social in nature; i.e. war, financial depressions, or overpopulation (p. 33). In arguing for "religious causes," the authors are saying that the doctrines of a religious group, as they are widely understood and taught, are causative in relation to conversion, whereas the previous understanding proposed they were associative. The implications of this are quite significant. If, as Stark and Finke maintain, the beliefs of a group are the main cause of conversions to that group, then it follows that the most fundamental aspect of religion is its conceptualization of the supernatural. One example of this is found on pp. 96-99 where the authors theorize that to the degree that a religion teaches that its god(s) are reliable, then to that degree will people be willing to wait until the afterlife to receive their reward (p. 96-99).

Next we see how these authors shape the idea that religious choices are rational choices. Until the 1970s and 80s, most social scientists followed a Durkheimian concept that explained religious conversion as the product of ideological appeal and general deviance. However the theory of "Rational Choice" in religions has forced a major rethinking of how we understand conversion. Stake and Finke produced what is now commonly referred to as Rational Choice (RC) theory. This is the idea that when making religious decisions,[26] people "weigh the anticipated rewards of a choice against its anticipated costs" (pp. 44-45). Driving the rational choice theory is a fundamental assumption of methodological individualism. In other words, social macro problems have to be solved at the level of individual choices, individuals who act purposefully, if we are to make sense of sociological phenomena (Bremmer, van Bekkum, and Molendijk, 2006 p. 15). Stark and Finke contend that despite the only recent application to religious behavior, using rational models to explain human behavior have long dominated the social sciences because it is possible to fashion far more powerful theories using this proposition than without it (*ibid*).

However, RC has not been without its critics. Steve Bruce (1999 pp. 121-125) argues that Rational Choice is fundamentally flawed because it tries to rationalize supernatural experiences, something the convert or religious adherent does not, nor feels required to do, in order to justify their faith. Kathryn Kraft (2007 p.83) also contests RC somewhat along the same line, or more specifically because she says it represents a non-religious appraisal of a decidedly religious experience, thus rendering it incapable of discerning the actual reasons for conversion or faith. Not only does RC have its critics, but there are also those building upon it, such as "Preferences,

---

[26] RC theory has been applied to many areas of life, but in this paper I will use it exclusively as Stark and Finke did, to refer to religious matters.

Constraints, and Choices in Religious Markets" by Darren E. Sherkat and John Wilson. (1995). However, space does not permit me to delve into this literature here.

One final theory from Stark and Finke that I will refer to in my own research is what they have called "religious economies" or the "economics of religion" (p.200-210). In the past, most theorists maintained that religious change occurred due to changing preferences in the individual or the society at large. Stark and Finke contest this, and argue that the demand side of a religious economy that is quite stable, rather it is changes in the *supply side* that sets-up the kind of religious changes we call conversion. This is important because it places critical importance in changing contextual factors, something that I have set out to understand through this research. I find this very helpful, however I do offer this critique. If taken too far, the theory of "economics of religion" places too much emphasis on those who make up the supply side, i.e. foreign missionary agents, and paints the convert into a passive position. While this does not appear to have been Stark and Finke's intent, it is certainly an error to be avoided in approaching this theory.

Moving on, it is worth looking at further work by Stark's original writing partner, John Loftand, who, together with Normon Skonovd, produced a very significant article, "Conversion Motifs" (1981). In this article, the authors continue with the same general trajectory as Lofland and Stark began with their landmark *American Sociological Review* article in 1965, but with important refinements.

Lofland and Skonovd assert that the wide differences in the way different theorists have conceptualized conversion is more than simply a difference in the theoretical positions of researchers, but are artifacts of the actual differences in the experiences of converts. They attempt to bring some order to the chaos by proposing an integrated model that accounts for both the subjective side of the converts experience as well as a more etic perspective, which a researcher often needs to take in order to make sense of what they have studied. The results are what Lofland and Skonovd call their six major motifs of conversion: Intellectual, Mystical, Experimental, Affectional, Revivalist, and Coercive. These are differentiated through a five point metric: degree of social pressure, temporal duration, level of affective arousal, affective content, and the belief-participation sequence of the convert. These variants attempt to account for a range of factors, focusing on the "intellectual, physical, and emotional" dynamics that are present during the conversion process. Each of these motifs is well developed, making the overall schema accessible as an analytical grid for other researchers.

Aside from the six motifs, which are the main thrust of the article, another point the authors make in the article is about how to account for the "conversion molding." One problem that researchers face is that converts may shape their stories to the accepted norms of the group which they have joined. While there is no way to intellectually eliminate this problem, Loftland and Skonovd state that it is minimized when we understand that the conversion experience is always shaped by expectations of what conversion is *supposed* to be like. Thus it is natural for a convert to sort out the "raw reality" of their experience in a way that fits with the paradigmatic accounts of their new group. Therefore, while the conversion narratives we actually access are shaped and filtered, they are still substantially accurate.

2.2.3 <u>Anthropological</u>

Now I consider that it is time to again move along my original continuum. Until now I have called it a movement from the philosophical and esoteric to the concrete. However, as has by now become obvious, a better way of labeling my little mental device would be as a movement from psychological studies on conversion, to sociological, and finally to anthropological.

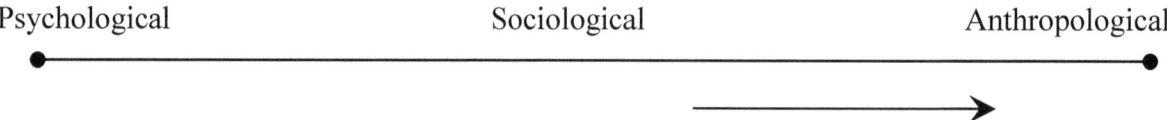

The primary reason for this move away from philosophical speculations is that I wish to take the actual beliefs of religious adherents seriously; and I find this most closely adheres with anthropological perspectives. It seems to me this is because anthropology has a tradition of placing higher value on the emic perspective than the other academic disciplines. The discipline of anthropology offers a prodigious amount of material about religious conversion; therefore, my choices of what to include or exclude were difficult. In the, end I chose three edited volumes and two fairly recent dissertations that were quite helpful.

I shall begin by looking at Robert Hefner's *Conversion to Christianity: Historical and Anthropological Perspectives on a Great Transformation* (1993). This book by Hefner is a classic among studies on the conversion process as it relates to Christianity. Although its contributors speak to various aspects of religious conversion across disciplinary boundaries, including anthropologists, sociologists, historians, and theologians, the focus is on the historical and anthropological. Hefner draws on conversion material scattered across several continents, and while the subject is always conversion *to* Christianity, it is about conversion *from* many different religions. As it pertains to my own thesis, there are a few areas of importance in Hefner's work.

First, the author combines the core ideas behind Stark and Finke's "Rational Choice" and "religious economies" theories (2000), although he reaches them by slightly different paths. As a parallel to Rational Choice theory, Hefner argues that with certain qualifications, Max Weber was right, traditional religions (ethnic religions) fail when challenged by world religions such as Christianity because "traditional religions are piecemeal in their approach to problems of meaning," whereas world religions offer "comprehensive responses to the ethical, emotional, and intellectual challenges of human life" (p. 7). Thus conversion to Christianity can be a thoroughly rational choice when one faces an increasingly complex world that their previous religion does not adequately explain. Then in a slightly different way of explaining the core of "religious economies," Hefner addresses the issue of religious conversion in intercultural encounters. He contends that when "a society is brought into contact with a larger political-economic order, institutions once vital for its subsistence" are often abolished or subverted. And when this happens, a "religion that promises a new measure of dignity and access to the values and rewards of the larger society may find a ready following among people previously committed to local ways" (pp. 26-27). This I found a powerful explanation of the situation in Central Asia when the Soviet order (including local islam) was crumbling and a new internationalist one (including globalized Christianity) was intruding.

Another insight that I found important comes from a later chapter, again written by the editor of the volume, on Christian conversion in Muslim Java. After identifying several factors in the local context, Hefner seems to almost stumble upon something that has much wider implications than the Javanese context. Through interviews with younger local converts, he discovered that Christianity was presented to them in a deeply personal form, and that "such ritually unmediated, individualized religiosity had no precedence in traditional village religion" (p. 116). Although he does not make this application, it is easy to see how this religiously inspired independence of thought could be very attractive in the context of globalization and expanding choices beyond their traditional world.

Another very important work on my short list is *The Anthropology of Religious Conversion* by Andrew Buckser and Stephen D. Glazier (2003). This work is the compilation of several anthropologists' covering current methodological, philosophical, and practical concerns of those studying religious conversion; however, these are embedded in case studies rather than explored as theories. Therefore, it was most helpful to see what some of the theories look like in field practice.

Although the entire book was excellent, it was worth reading if only for page one of the introduction, where contributor Diane Austin-Broos offers one of the best, most succinct definitions of conversion I have yet to see. She calls religious conversion "a form of passage, a 'turning from and to' that is neither syncretism nor absolute breach" (p. 1). Austin-Broos goes on to elaborate that rather than a simple voiding of the past self, conversion is a passage that often involves reorienting of new practices, while attempting to stay within the same national culture.

This "neither syncretism nor absolute breach" is also a tantalizing hint of why world Christianity[27] has become one of the world's largest "transnational milieus" rather than simply another colonizing process (p. 3).

Another contributor, Robert Anderson, raises the point that the term 'conversion' itself is culture bound, the product of Abramic faiths, thus possibly valid in other contexts (p. 124). If Anderson's idea is properly qualified, it is both accurate and important. Since Islam offers no paradigm for switching to another faith other than apostasy[28], a decidedly negative image, then it is unsurprising that converts often attempt to fit their experiences into the accepted paradigm of their new faith community, thus supporting the application of Loftland and Skonovd's ideas (1981) to my research context. But further implications of this fascinating topic must wait until later in this paper.

To continue the review of *The Anthropology of Religious Conversion*, I would look at a chapter by Roger Lohamann. This author theorizes that at the core of much religion is "a sense of social relationship with imaginary[29] supernatural beings (p. 119). Thus religious conversion is perhaps best understood as "taking on a relationship with new supernatural beings," and that acceptance of new beliefs or dogmas is "often a secondary consequence" (pp. 117-118). Taking into account the concerns about Lohamann's pejorative above, I generally agree with his analysis except that he goes too far when asserting that conversion is also the "abandonment of one set of

---

[27] Lamin Sanneh (2003) uses "world Christianity" to refer to a multi-cultural expression of Christianity on the world stage, as opposed to "global Christianity," which he uses to refer to those expressions of the same faith which are fundamentally rooted in the traditions and denominations of the Western missionary experience.
[28] See review of "Apostasy" by Ibn Warraq later in this chapter.
[29] I strongly object to the author's use of the term 'imaginary' here, as not only is it out of place as an etic perspective in an article proposing to present the emic, but it also has the feeling of being used as a pejorative in this case.

relationships...and their replacement with a new set (p. 119). He would have done well to read Austin-Broos introduction to the volume because "abandonment" and "replacement" are far too strong of words to accurately describe the social changes in many, if not most conversions.

And finally, I would review *Religious Conversion in India: Modes, Motivations, and Meanings* edited by Rowena Robinson and Sathianathan Clarke (2003). Robinson and Clarke's work is different from the two previous because it has a geographic focus, the Indian sub-continent, and delves deeply into the cultural and historical issues that form the context of conversions there.

Unlike many other anthropological works, Robinson and Clarke start by offering theory that will frame the more field-grounded chapters later in the volume. They theorize that all religious conversions entail, at the least, "three interlocking and interdependent dominant symbols: God, world, and human beings (p. 3). Thus conversion can be explained as the experience of a person revisiting and remixing these elements, so that their relationships are more acceptable to the convert than they were before (*ibid*). There are several benefits of this tripartite conversion model. One, it is quite straightforward and unpretentious, in some ways reminding the reader of Lewis Rambo's "four essential components of conversion" (1993). Another value in the Robinson-Clarke model is that it helps move conversion to Christ away from the stereotypical "Damascus road" experience of Saul of Tarsus, and places it in a broader family of human experiences. The editors remark that "conversion is a range of possibilities" including both the dramatic as well as the more gradual (p. 8).

In a later chapter, Clarke looks very specifically at conversion to Christianity. He makes several observations that may play a role in my analysis. She notes that sometimes when groups of people chose to relate to their pre-conversion symbolic world differently, it may be due to issues of status and power that they previously had, or did not have, as the case may be. For example, high caste Hindu converts to Christianity often bring symbols of Brahmic Hinduism into their new faith, whereas Dalits [outcastes] and tribals do not (pp. 289-290).

Also, Clarke agrees with others I have already reviewed such as Austin-Broos (2003), or Hefner (1993) when she describes how the Christian converts in Goa mediated their new faith through accommodation of their previous one, and negotiation with the demands of the new, rather than simply eliminating their indigenous ways (p. 314). This would predict the likelihood that we will also see such accommodation and negotiation in Central Asia, a situation where missionaries have had far less political and legal power.

And finally, Clarke deals with the case of Indian Dalits, and *out caste,* which have traditionally been considered Hindu, but are more accurately described as Animists, practicing various, related ethnic religions. In this case, the author outlines how conversion for this group was clearly part of a collective effort to locate itself in a different symbolic universe, one that did not justify and support the oppression its people face as an outcaste community according to the Hindu worldview (pp. 337-338). The relevance of this point is that there are several ways in which Central Asians might see conversion to Christ in a similar fashion, as an attempt to define themselves with different symbols thus changing their personal value[30]. The author also points out through the conversion of the Dalits that we do well to avoid the "Orientalist's pitfall which accentuates the agency of the western agents, whether colonial or missionary, and devalues the instrumentality of the native subjects [converts] themselves" (p. 336).

In order to wrap-up this lengthy section on anthropological literature on conversion in general, I will discuss two fairly recent PhD dissertations that I found particularly helpful, *A Religious Paradigm Shift for Adult Spaniards in The Conversion Process to Evangelical Christianity* by Jeffrey Turnbough (2004), and *Personal Transformation and Religious Faith: A Narrative Approach to Conversion by* Elizabeth E. Dufault-Hunter (2005). I will begin with Turnbough.

Turnbough associates the conversion process for Spaniards to a paradigm shift, a change in their worldview. After exploring definitions of the term "worldview," he draws on the work of Thomas Kuhn (1996) that makes religious conversion analogous to the kind of paradigm shift that happens during scientific revolutions. He suggests that such paradigm shifts happen when at least two criteria are met: issues arise, or are recognized, which cause anxiety because the existing paradigm cannot answer them; and secondly, there must appear a new paradigm that holds the promise of doing so. It is quite easy to see how this might apply to religious conversion.

---

[30] Two points of clarification are in order. First, whereas Clarke documents that the Dalits having made this move collectively, I am not suggesting the same has or will happen collectively in Central Asia. Secondly, at this point this is pure speculation; therefore, I will not give any greater details until and unless the interviews themselves support this theory.

Also, Turnbough contends that Spain is a perfect example of a situation where religious practice is low, yet religious pluralism is only *de jure*, because the majority of the population refuses to accept pluralism as social reality. Therefore, the paradigm of a particular religious belief becomes the dominant social paradigm as well, thus guaranteeing a context of hostility and even persecution for those who would dare to convert (p. 150). He goes even further by asserting that in a society with low levels of religious observance, the only logical explanation for strong negative social reactions against conversion is that they are seen not as individual actions or beliefs but as shifts against the prevailing paradigm, something typically associated with high resistance (p. 201).

Finally, although on the surface, Turnbough's research concerns religious conversion in a very different environment than my own, a deeper reading points to important similarities that make this an important work for me to review. Early in the research he notes that although Spain offers legal protection for religious conversion, it is still a country marked by a "homogeneous culture in which one predominant religion exists" and in which it is "socially and culturally unacceptable to convert, especially to a drastically different religion." I found it fascinating that the author concluded that conversions from Islam to Christianity closely paralleled his own observations in Spain, an eerie echo of the context of my own study, which I will explore later.

The next thesis that I found very insightful concerning the general topic of conversion was by Elizabeth E. Dufault-Hunter, *Personal Transformation and Religious Faith: A Narrative Approach to Conversion* (2005). I found Ms. Dufault-Hunter's research particularly interesting because while it was located worlds away from my own, Los Angeles verses Central Asia, it shares a close methodological similarity to the plan and values that inform my own research. The work is the product of in-depth interviews with American converts to the Nation of Islam. Her entire approach is shaped around a commitment to Grounded Research and narrative review methodology for many reasons, not least of which is because through narrative we can discover the living beliefs and practices that make up a religion, rather than "beliefs [which] can be so disembodied" by other methods of religious/ethical research (pp. 20-21).

The author argues that due to its "inherently storied nature, religious conversion must be read through a narrative lens" (p. vii), and later in the thesis, makes a strong case for this assertion. The author contends that narrative can help us understand the motivations behind a person's conversion (p. 96), that it shows us how people make meaning of their religious identities (p. 97), and that it may even be the vital key to understanding the difference between cognitive statements about religion and the living faith of converts (*ibid*). Default-Hunter contends that rather than "demythologizing faith" with Durkheim, we need to engage in more narrative inquiry of religion because it helps us understand the power of a person's story. Through narrative, conversion becomes more than adherence to new social norms; it is transformed into the rewriting of a person's own story (p. 155-158). Case in point, the alternate African-American narrative offered by the nation of Islam became the basis of a completely new personal narrative for converts. They discarded a personal narrative of "bitches, whores and niggers" (p. 155) for a metanarrative in which black people were "once [a] great people—the source of all civilization" (p. 154). Default-Hunter suggests that whether outsiders consider a religious metanarrative to be myth, spiritualized truth, or factual history, it has the power, through conversion, to become woven into the convert's own story. Perhaps this is the essence of religious conversion? Certainly it will be most helpful in understanding conversion stories from Central Asia.

2.2 Literature Related to Muslim Conversions to Christianity

There is a growing corpus of studies about Muslim conversions to Christianity, the majority of which are written from a Christian missionary perspective. While "missionary research" is by nature sectarian, not all of it is overly prejudiced. I found a number of well-written, scholarly works that are most suitable for my purposes. That said, the first work I will review is a book with obvious biases *against* Christianity[31], *Leaving Islam: Apostates Speak Out* by Ibn Warriq (2003). Despite his general disdain of all things religious, the author offers important insights into Muslim conversions to Christianity, embedded in a much larger work concerning conversion *from* Islam *to* almost anything else.

Perhaps the book's most significant contribution to this discussion is a stark reminder that in order to build an emic understanding of conversion *from* Islam, we must set-aside the values-neutral, relativistic framework that is common in Western academia. In the Islamic world, a person does not choose a faith in the way he chooses a political party or profession. Rather, conversion from Islam is, first and foremost, an act of *apostasy*.

There are, of course, several implications of viewing conversion this way, but a very important one is only hinted at in the book. Since conversion is apostasy—not choice—then it is

---

[31] Warriq's general anti-religious bias is of little consequence to the points that I will review; therefore, I will not delineate or rebut any of his views.

a moral issue, and morality is usually dealt with by society not government. Regrettably, Warriq all but ignores this important distinction. For example, the antagonists who pressure converts to return to Islam or engage in outright persecution are never clearly identified by Warriq, thus giving the impression that Muslim society and Islamic governments are synonymous in this regard. While that may have been true in times long past[32], it is patently untrue in the 21st Century. Furthermore, by projecting a unary relationship between society and state, Warriq distorts perceptions about the ramifications of conversion from Islam, thus distorting our ideas of conversion itself.

This is part and parcel of a larger issue, that *Leaving Islam* paints a picture of conversion that is clearly polemical. If someone were to read Warriq alone to understand conversion from Islam, they would deduce that there is an almost universal death penalty for apostasy, despite the fact that there is "a great variety of 'Muslim voices'" on the matter of human rights (Bielefeldt, 1995 p. 587). Furthermore, *Leaving Islam* seems to ignore the reality that the Islamic world is changing in profound and unpredictable ways, and that "many Muslims are reconsidering the doctrine of apostasy (Peters & DeVries, 1977 p. 25). While Muslim authorities, in several countries, have often ruled that known Communists are apostates, public opinion has never sided with them (Peters & DeVries, 1977 pp. 21-22). These hint toward the reality in Post-Soviet Central Asia that the "punishment" for apostasy is much more a social, rather than judicial, matter.

---

[32] This does not mean that I necessarily agree with Warriq's view of the relationship between state and society in the Islamic past; that is well beyond the scope of this thesis.

Nevertheless, despite its flaws, Warriq's work is well worth reading, particularly because it gives a great deal of attention to the actual words of apostates, not just the analysis of them. This raises an important point. Despite the fact that most scholars classify Islam as a religion of orthopraxy, i.e. correct practice, apostasy appears to often be verbal and confessional, not behavioral (pp. 16 & 28). This could have significant implications in the way converts tell their stories.

Another insightful book dealing with Muslim conversions is *From the Straight Path to the Narrow Way,* edited by my good friend David Greenlee (2005). This selection is a significant contribution to understanding the context, meaning, and methods of conversion that are currently part of the interaction between Christian missions and Muslim peoples. Aside from case studies and a few highly theological chapters, the book deals with several issues of interest for scholars of religious studies. These range from the transformation of worldview and identity continuity, to factors leading to conversion among Central Asian Muslims—written by a Central Asian convert no less.

For example, Paul Hiebert looks at the interaction between religious conversion and worldview. He maintains that even in those cases where conversion seems swift or sudden, at the worldview level it is more of a gradual shift over time as the person finds that a new belief system answers their critical questions better than their natal one. (pp. 27-28).

In another chapter, Greenlee and contributor Rick Love outline several lenses through which we often view conversion, including psychological, behavioral, sociological, and cultural (pp. 38-49). The importance of this discussion is not the individual lenses, nor the comprehensiveness of the list, but rather that there are multiple lenses through which we can view conversion, and each of them plays a part in understanding the conversion experience.

Another contributor, Mary McVicker, writes about supernatural experiences of women converts. Without dismissing the claim of actual supernatural occurrences, she focuses on these reports as "multisensory" experiences (p.129). She argues that the combination of physical sensations and certain behavioral experiences while with other converts, can sometimes be the trigger to conversion because these are forms of "experiential knowledge," which is the preferred learning style of South Asian women (pp. 132-132). While it should be noted that like Warriq's *Leaving Islam,* Greenlee's volume has an agenda, [33] but thankfully it is lacking the animus that seeps through Warriq's work.

Now I will shift my attention to some of the recent academic works that make up the small, but growing body of dissertations and theses being written on the topic of Muslim conversions to Christ. To begin, I will examine one that seems to be one of the first PhD dissertations written on this topic, *Christian Conversion From Islam* (1996), written by the same David Greenlee reviewed above, as he studied Muslim conversions in Morocco.

Greenlee found that several of the converts he interviewed were, at least initially, more attracted to the foreignness of the Christian message than to the message itself (pp. 109-121). This is likely explained by the relationship between globalization Christianity in post-colonial environments (van der Veer, 1996 pp. 6-7), and/or theories about how people who are

---

[33] In Greenlee's work, conversion to Christianity is clearly the goal. On the other hand, Warriq seems to want Muslims to convert to *anything* else, although arguably he would greatly prefer that conversion be to some form of secular humanism.

dissatisfied with their culture are more likely to be open to foreign cultural values, including the radical step of conversion to a competing religion (Rambo, 1993), (Gooren, 2007), (Radford, 2011). Also, Greenlee observed that when a person who has had little or no prior contact with Christianity, his conversion is likely to be experienced as a gradual process, not a crisis point (p. 134-136), although Greenlee seemed to have little actual data to support this.

And finally, Greenlee offers what he calls "the basic pattern of conversion," which is the convert's interaction with national Christians from a similar Muslim background (p. 92). I am very interested to see if Greenlee's assertion about the significance of interaction with other Muslim converts will show-up in the interviews I will collect.

Moving on, I am most fortunate that one of the better academic studies done on this topic during the past decade was written by a friend and colleague, David Radford, and that his work has some close parallels to my own research. Radford's work is entitled, *Religious Conversion and the Reconstruction of Ethnic Identity* (2011). Radford conducted a mixed-methods study of conversion among ethnic Kyrgyz, all living in their titular state. His data is drawn from 49 interviews and 427 responses to a survey (p. 76).

The thrust of Radford's thesis is that conversion to Christianity is happening in such a way among the Kyrgyz that it is challenging their concept of identity (pp. 132-133). With the Soviet Union in the rearview mirror, many Kyrgyz found themselves in need of reconstructing their identity. And although Kyrgyz have usually considered Islam an intrinsic plank of their ethnic identity (p. 19), for some Kyrgyz, the inclusion of Christianity was an acceptable innovation (p. 143).

Another important factor that Radford uncovers in his research is the relationship between conversion and the seeking of spiritual power. He explains that for the majority of "Muslims" he surveyed, Animism played a significant role in their worldview (p. 141). Therefore, it is not surprising that a different religious message, in this case a version of Christianity that contained elements of spiritual power, made quick inroads.

Radford's work is very contemporary and relevant to my own research; nevertheless, there is clear and major divergence in both our methodology and study populations. Therefore, I expect that there will be both similarities and significant differences in our findings.

Another study that focused on the covert's identity, but this time in the Arab world, is *Community and Identity Among Arabs of a Muslim Background who Choose to Follow A Christian Faith* by Kathryn A. Kraft (2007). As may be surmised by the title, the author spends the majority of her time focusing on the social dimension of conversion, and by extension, on one of the major implications of this, the convert's personal identity.

Kraft supports the use of Grounded Theory because theories that are common in religious studies have often "obscured many of the rich and significant changes happening in society around the world that do not fit into the Western-centric models developed so far (2007 p. 84). While this is certainly true at one level, it is also the location of one of the few flaws I found in her thinking. Several times Kraft disputes the validity of using conversion theories related to New Religious Movements (NRMs) to understand Muslim conversions. She is right in contending that the pluralistic West is a very different context from the Islamic world; however, as David Radford points out, Protestant groups are the New Religious Movements in Central

Asia (Radford, 2008 p. 12-13). Therefore theories such as those by Lofland and Stark (1965) or Stark and Finke (2000) are often very insightful.

Kraft found that a number of people in her study first learned about the Christian faith as they were attempting to steer a friend or relative away from Christianity. But the more they studied, the more they became attracted to Christian beliefs (pp. 96-97). This seems to fit with at least some of the preliminary interviews I have done in Central Asia. I am, however, not satisfied with Kraft's conclusions on this matter, as she finds this pathway to conversion to be primarily relational, that the antagonists became converts because of the personal connection with the Christian they were previously trying to dissuade. I find her argument unconvincing, and hope to find better explanations in my own data when the cases are similar.

Another study in an Arab context that focused on Identity of Muslim converts to Christ was done by Jens Barnett. While the full dissertation is not available, I was able to find a conference paper in which he presented his major findings: *Conversion's Consequences: Identity, Belonging, and Hybridity amongst Muslim Followers of Christ in the Kingdom of Jordan* (2008).

Perhaps the most important contribution to the field from Barnett's thesis is its focus on the development of a "hybrid" identity, part Christian and part Muslim. The author Barnett reasons this is possible because identities have "fuzzy boundaries" which enable the person to be members of two or more groups at one time[34] (p. 20). Thus, the cultural "hybrid" lives in a third

---

[34] Here Barnett is drawing significantly from Paul Hiebert's work, particularly "Conversion, Culture, and Cognitive Categories (1978) and "The Category 'Christian' in the Mission Task" (1983).

space, a place where seemingly irreconcilable cultural differences are allowed to dialogue and even remain in unresolved ambiguity. These allow the convert to anchor his personality to multiple points, sequentially as well as simultaneously, thus forming a unique identity construction (p. 5). Barnett found that converts who take this path often use behaviors as a form of cultural camouflage, one kind when with Christians, with whom they share a belief, and one with Muslims, under whose cultural power they live (p. 10). However, even Barnett acknowledges there are limits to "hybridity" (p.15), particularly as it concerns the surrounding community, but their community sees them in something confirmed by McBrien and Pelkmans in Central Asia (2008).

A final study that I found helpful is about Muslim conversions to Christianity in a tiny autonomous province of the former Soviet state of Georgia, *Baptized Georgian: Religious Conversion to Christianity in Autonomous Ajaria* by Mathijs Pelkmans (2005).

In this study the author found that the crumbling of state-sponsored communism allowed a "flexible space" to emerge in which religious experimentation could take place (p. 3). As it became increasingly obvious that the Soviet state ideology has failed them, Muslims became more and more open to change, not only in the realm of economics, but in all of life's interrelated systems, which of course include religion. However, to attribute the development of this conversion "space" completely to the collapse of Soviet ideology would be a gross simplification.

Among many factors Pelkmans' explores, he notes that Christianity came to be a proxy for progress in the eyes of many Muslims in Ajaria (p. 26). There were several reasons for this, one being a linkage between higher education and Christianity (p. 18). Unfortunately Pelkmans does not explore the reasons these became linked in the minds of Ajarian Muslims. Also, he hypothesizes that another important reason for the linkage is that both Christianity and modernity place high value in change, thus Christian conversion has the potential to become symbolic of general personal renewal, not just religious change (p. 26).

Pelknams was clearly unsatisfied with some of the reasons converts gave for their religious choices (p. 19). For example, some people explained their choice to become Christian through reconnecting with historic identities: "I was baptized because the first Georgians were Christians, so that is our religion," or matters of family solidarity: "everyone else in my family became Christian, that is how I became convinced that Christianity is the true religion" (*ibid*). The fact that these answers perplexed him perhaps tells us more about the assumptions of Western researchers than it does about the converts themselves.

2.3 Literature Related to the Context of Islam in post-Soviet Central Asia

The final grouping of literature that must be reviewed is that which primarily relates to my thesis in the matter of context. In this section of the review, I will briefly survey the literature concerning Islam in post-Soviet Central Asia. In the first few years after the terrorist attacks known in short as 9/11, there was a sudden flourish of books on Central Asia. While most of these centered on Afghanistan and Pakistan, some ventured into topics farther north. Representative of these is *Jihad: The Rise of Militant Islam in Central Asia* by Ahmed Rashid, a respected scholar with solid knowledge of Islam in Pakistan and Afghanistan, yet who is clearly out of his depth in the post-Soviet context, where he relies on undependable secondhand sources and demonstrates a very unsophisticated grasp of Soviet history in the region. Thus, Rashid's *Jihad* is distinctly sub-par and not worth reviewing for this thesis[35]. I have mentioned it only because it is unfortunately well known. Thankfully, there are other lesser-known works on Central Asia that are solid work of qualified academics. Unsurprisingly, the first English books on anything post-Soviet were those written by Russian scholars, and this is true for Central Asia.

Chronologically, perhaps the first of these is a translated volume by Sergei Poliakov (with Martha Brill Olcott), *Everyday Islam: Religion and Tradition in Central Asia* (1992). Poliakov was an anthropologist from Moscow State University who studied Central Asian Muslims for more than three decades. Martha Olcott worked to bring a slimmed down version of his *magnum opus* to English because she believed it contained "a great wealth of information… made accessible to readers of English for the first time" (p. xix). Poliakov reviews his field observations from many trips to the region and was particularly concerned with the economic impact of continued adherence to Islamic patterns of life among Soviet citizens. A full two-thirds of the book is devoted to economic topics such as "Traditionalism and the Economic Structure" (pp. 23-31) or "The Family Budget" (pp. 87-92). Poliakov was particularly interested in the way Islamic traditions produced "non-rational" economic behavior. Ultimately, Poliakov comes to the sweeping conclusion that the mosque and other religious institutions in the region are the *de facto* governors of all behavior for Central Asians (p. 99).

---

[35] Rashid is clearly a well-informed scholar of the Afghan-Pakistani region, but is just as clearly out of his depth in post-Soviet space. He places far too great a weight on shared ancient history and geography, which causes him to apparently assume that 70+ years of Soviet rule Central Asia was of no greater impact than the brief Soviet occupation of Afghanistan.

Although the author gives us a detailed picture of Islam at the transitional moment between the Soviet Union and the newly independent states, Poliakov's bias as a Soviet era scholar is quite strong. A good example of this is when he writes, "conversations on the subject [of trade] with a very wide circle of people, suggest that for the majority…a Central Asian and a speculating profiteer[36] are synonymous" (p. 33). The stature of Poliakov's work is raised by Martha Olcott's involvement in the project, notwithstanding her criticism of his "caustic critique of Islamic traditionalism" (p. xxvi). However, the involvement of a political scientist like Martha Olcott in an ethnographic work reminds us that until most recently, political studies have dominated studies on post-Soviet Central Asia (Rasuly-Paleczek, 2005 p.3).

Another example of early post-Soviet thinking on Islam in Central Asia comes in the form of an edited volume by Dale Eickelman, *Russia's Muslim Frontiers* (1993). This book is the result of attempts by US scholars to interact with late- and post-Soviet Russian academics, with contributing authors from both sides of the Cold War divide. And while much of this volume leans toward geopolitical analysis, it still contains work that shed much light on the religious situation in contemporary Central Asia.

One very insightful chapter is titled "Islam and Communism: The Experience of Coexistence," written by Alexei Malashenko, a specialist in Oriental religions at the Russian Academy of Sciences in Moscow. The thesis of this chapter is best framed by the question, "did Muslim societies within the former Soviet Union lose their religiousity (sic)?" (p. 63). Malashenko begins by arguing that since "the Bolsheviks—including V.I. Lenin—always

---

[36] For those unfamiliar with the context of Soviet economics, the term "speculator" was often paired with "capitalist pig!" during the Soviet era in Central Asia (Hussan A. 2004).

showed caution in matters concerning the Muslim East," the pattern was set for successive Soviet administrations, so that they never brought as great a pressure on the Islamic regions as they could have (*ibid*). He also contends that the relative geographic isolation of Central Asia, and indigenous kinship structures made it much harder for the security services to establish the same kind of control that they exercised elsewhere in the country (p. 64). Based on these and other reasons, Malashenko contends that despite an ambiguous official status, "Islam remained the preserver of spirituality, the framework for a worldview, and, to a significant extent, the regulator of relations between people" (p. 66) in Central Asia. Poliakov and Malashenko are representative of a discernible trend among Soviet-era Russian scholars who see Islam in Central Asia as undefeated by 70 years of Maxist rule. As I shall later point out, this opinion is strongly contested.

Another edited volume that attempts to access Russian expertise while providing outside perspective is *Muslim Eurasia: Conflicting Legacies*, edited by Israeli scholar Yaacov Ro'i. The best chapters are those written by Ro'i himself, particularly chapter one, "The Secularization of Islam in the USSR's Muslim Areas."

Ro'i points out that while there was a general trend toward secularization of Muslim societies after the collapse of the Ottoman Empire after World War I, the process was much more severe in Central Asia. The reason for this was that from the earliest times of the Bolshevik revolution, Islam in Central Asia was repressed, because it was feared that it would eventually link-up with pan-Islamic or pan-Turkic movements. Also, the process of secularization was different in Soviet Muslim territories. In nearby Muslim lands such as Turkey, secularization was an internal response to a perceived failure of Islam, but in Central Asia the grinding down of Islam's dominance over life was driven from without, by ethnically different people (pp. 5-6).

Ro'i suggests that the Soviet authorities must have been cognizant of the backward, traditionalist nature of Islam in the region because their strongest attacks were against the reformers of the *Jadid* movement[37] during the 1930s, since the *Jadids* wanted to modernize Islam, and that would have thwarted the obvious Soviet design to slowly strangle Islam so it would atrophy and die an apparently natural death (p. 8). Ro'i maintains that the sophistication and brutality of the Soviet anti-religious policy completed a process begun by traditionalism in Central Asia. Soviet policy reshaped Islam, as practiced in Soviet domains, into little more than a collection of folk ways and life-cycle rituals (p. 9).

However, Ro'i is clear that this intense Soviet pressure against Islam did not destroy it, but rather reshaped it, and the author does a good job of elucidating the differences between these two concepts. For example, after arguing that Islam was "subdued" by the Soviets, he then moves into analysis similar to Poliakov (1998) in suggesting that "as a way of life that is designed to embody certain beliefs and dogmas, Islam is not by definition, and cannot be, cut off (*sic*) from everyday life" (p. 11). Then the author compiles significant evidence that extensive underground Islamic societies existed even after several decades of government repression. For example, in the 1960s the Soviet government was fully aware that there were six times as many "unofficial, unregistered Muslim groups, with their own Imam" as there were official, registered ones. Then, in the mid-1980s, a study by the Soviet Academy of Social Sciences found

---

[37] *Jadid* is English shorthand for the *usul-I jadid*, a new method of teaching Arabic to children in the local school system. It became a movement during the early Russian colonial era of Central Asia.

"comparatively extensive practice of [Islamic] traditions, festivals and rites among all socio-demographic groups of population" (pp. 13-14). Yet in testimony to the impact of the anti-religious purges, that same study also found that Islamic "religious leaders had little or no religious training, and who clearly based their leadership role on folk practices" (p. 15).

In a chapter on Soviet language policy, Kreindler discusses an important, yet often overlooked issue of native language script. While Soviet language policy overwhelmingly favored native languages until the time of Khrushchev (p. 195), Soviet authorities changed the written forms of their native languages from Arabic script, first to Latin, then later to Cyrillic script (p. 192). This would have profound implications, not only in helping make the learning of Russian easier, but also to effectively cut off Muslims from textual interaction with the larger Islamic world. Furthermore, Kreindler points out that while "non-Russian children continued to receive a great part of their schooling in the mother tongue" the creative side of non-Russian languages was under assault as "native language writers and linguists, teachers and actors were being swept away in purges" (p. 165). While this certainly was part of larger policy goals to bring about stagnation of Muslim cultures, Kreindler perceptively argues that overall, Soviet policy first included, but later alienated, many Muslims in Soviet lands.

And as a final review in this final section, I will look at what I consider the most significant recent book on this topic, *Islam After Communism: Religion and Politics in Central Asia* by Adeeb Khalid (2007). While this author offers a generally similar picture of post-Soviet Islam as does Ro'i, he goes further and argues that the late Islamic religious knowledge in post-Soviet Central Asia has much deeper roots than Soviet policies. Khalid contends that even "before to the Russian conquest, for the bulk of the population, being Muslim meant being part of a community that saw itself as Muslim. It had little to do with mastery, by every individual, of the basic textual sources of Islam" (p. 21). This is an important point for researchers who, like myself, have the hyper-individualism of modern Protestantism as a general religious framework.

This leads Khalid to contend that Islam in Central Asian Islam has always been quite different from Islam in other areas, which fits with his general framework that there is not any one normative Islam, only local *islams* which share certain normative features across time and space (p. 23). In this the author seems to be on solid ground and firmly within the anthropological tradition of Getz. However, I would seriously question the final destination of this line of reasoning, in which Khalid maintains that "the answer to the question of who speaks for Islam is that any Muslim may speak on behalf of Islam" (p. 24). This seems much more derived from the postmodernist intellectualism of American universities that from the worldview of the Central Asians I have known over the past fifteen years.

In constructing a historical framework for his views, Khalid highlights the importance of understanding the *Jadid* movement, particularly because they believed that Islam was more a set of sociopolitical ideas than a religion. The *Jadids* taught that true Islam was found in direct access to the scriptural sources of Islam, the Quran and hadiths, without the aid of the commentaries and comments of centuries of scholars (p.41). This sounds quite reasonable to many in the West, particularly since it shares certain characteristics with Protestant Christianity[38]. Khalid insightfully reasons that by emphasizing Arabic language literacy as a functional skill,

---

[38] In particular, *Jadids* and Protestants share a focus on source texts and individual interpretation, specifically in opposition to the teachings of the older, traditional sources of religious authority.

rather than a sacred activity, the *Jadids* were challenging established patterns of cultural authority. "Much of the Ulama's authority rested in their command of the tradition of interpretation of the sacred texts of Islam" (p. 43), thus when the *Jadids* taught reading outside of their control it was almost as dangerous as translating the Bible into English had been in Reformation era England.

Also, Khalid demonstrates keen perception when he suggests that service in the Soviet armies during World War II transformed the individual identities of Muslims across the region. Like some kind of watershed, Uzbeks, Tatar, and Kazakhs left home as peasants, but returned from the war as Soviet citizens. The war became a central node of pan-Soviet identity and collective memory, a major aspect of collective identity that Muslims shared with non-Muslims (p. 77). Perhaps this, more than any intentional efforts of the Soviet authorities, explains the depth of *Sovietization* experienced by Central Asian Muslims of the past generation. And while it is likely the later generations may not feel it quite as keenly, public participation in holidays such as Victory Day (May 9) surely brought their children and grandchildren into the same orb.

The core of Khalid's thesis is that the destructive force of the Soviet regime's long-running attack on Islam was virtually unprecedented in the history of the religion. "In the history of Central Asia, the fury of the regime's attack on Islam and its institutions is comparable perhaps only to that of Genghis Khan, whose conquest of the region seven centuries earlier had caused massive destruction and long-term transformations in religious culture," and while Islam survived then, as now, it was "transformed in many ways." Most devastating to the religion was that "the Soviet assault destroyed the means through which Islamic knowledge was produced and transmitted" (pp. 81-82). To Khalid, the importance of this can hardly be overstated. This attack at the root of Islamic knowledge caused a migration of religious identity from scriptural sources to ethnic ones. Thus Islam became a meta-ethnic grouping, similar to the designation "Turkic," rather than a religious tradition that is practiced or understood (p. 83).

By now it is obvious that Khalid's view[39] of Central Asian Islam as a house devastated and disfigured is dramatically different from that of Malashenko (1993) or Poliakov (1998) who see it as unbowed. I find it both interesting and insightful that representative of the two sides of this debate stand a Muslim scholar from the US and a Russian from Moscow. Ironically, this reminds me of a comment of Dale Eickelman, in the closing chapter of *Russia's Muslim Frontiers* where Mohammad Masud writes about this very topic. He states that although the common Muslim complaint that non-Muslims cannot understand Islam (hence critique it) is weak and self-serving, the background of the scholar doing the critique is of vital importance, particularly their cultural literacy, nationality, religious background and worldview (1993 p. 198).

2.4 Locating this Research Vis-à-vis the Literature

Before going any further it is important to clarify how this study relates to this extensive body of existing literature. To that I will now turn. There are several theories with which I will extensively interact in this research. To begin, Grounded Theory (GT) (Glasser & Strauss 1967)

---

[39] Khalid and Ro'i are in significant agreement about how Islam faired under Communism; however, for three reasons, I see Khalid as the best representative of this view. One, he explores the situation in much more detail; two, he carries us into the post-Soviet era; and three, he unpacks the implications of a disfigured Islam in Central Asia, something that Ro'i does not do.

has had a large impact on the way I have approached this subject. GT states that we should expect plausible explanations (i.e. theories) to be found in the data itself, thus requiring the researcher to focus on interpreting the data rather than seeking to apply external theories. However, although Grounded Theory significantly shapes this research, there are limits. For example, even though I have been careful to place data before theory, there are existing theories that so clearly address the data I have collected that they cannot be ignored. In particular, Stark and Finke's theory of "religious economies" (2000) resonates with my data set. This is because the theory of religious economies posits that conversions are usually the result in changes on the "supply side" of religion, i.e. changes in the socio-religious context, and as I have stressed, context is critically important to this study. In taking this position, I have consciously located this project in close conceptual proximity to anthropological approaches to conversion such as Hefner (2000), Buckser and Glazier (2003), and Robinson and Clarke (2003). However, while the above authors demonstrate an appreciation for the people who actually experienced what is being discussed and analyzed, they still tend to keep their words at a distance; in this I will significantly diverge. In this study I have used a Narrative Inquiry approach, which focuses on generating meaning by carefully analyzing individuals' self-narratives (Lieblich, Tuval-Mashiach, & Zilber, 1998). However, I have also been careful to balance this with the realization that these self-narratives can only be understood in light of their post-Soviet Central Asian context. As regarding the context, my work is most closely aligned with that of Adeeb Khalid (2007), who argues persuasively that the *islam* which Central Asians converted from is a severely localized version which has few of the attributes which we normally associate with the powerful world religion Islam.

However, even here I will slightly diverge from Khalid because of what I perceive as a creeping resurgence of universal Islam in the area[40].

Chapter 3 - Methodology

In order to understand the methodological choices I have made, we must first revisit the purpose of this study, which are two-fold. One, to learn what the personal narratives of Muslim converts to Christ in post-Soviet Central Asia tell us about emic understandings of conversion. And two, how contextual factors have influenced the way these conversions are experienced. In order to explore this in the widest possible way, my research has been guided by the following question:

<u>What do the conversion narratives of Muslim converts to Christ in post-Soviet Central Asia tell us about the way they understand their conversion, the contextual influences on their conversions, and about the nature of religious conversion itself?</u>

The sensitivity of this question plus the challenges of the field context created a number of challenges and contributed to the way I developed my methodology for researching this thesis. In order to explain my methodological choices, I will start with the structure of this chapter. First, I will explain my research approach, paradigm, and rationale. Second, I will explain how I approached sampling, and thus drew my study population. Third, I will deal with matters of

---

[40] It is quite possible that Khalid misses this point because the phenomena was only in its embryonic stages when he did his research. However, it is clear that on the ground in Central Asia, universal Islam is on the global menu people are encountering, just as I have argued Protestant Christianity is.

research design, looking at both data collection methods and data analysis. I will finish this chapter with sections on ethical considerations, reliability of the findings, and study limitations.

3.1 Theoretical Paradigm

This study is based on the theoretical paradigm usually referred to as Social Constructivism. This approach asserts that the human world is fundamentally different from the natural, physical world thus requiring a fundamentally different approach to its study. Social Constructivism challenges the traditional ontology of empirical science, that there is a single reality existing independent of any observer's perspective, with an ontology that asserts multiple, socially constructed realities which have real consequences because it is through those realities that people perceive their world (Guba & Lincoln 1989, p. 84). A good example of this theory, and its rational limits, comes from Michael Crotty when he reasons:

> "[A] tree" is clearly a commonly agreed-on category of plant life in North America. From an objective point of view we would say there is only one reality we call a tree. Nevertheless, it is likely that the term will carry very different connotations to people living in a logging town, an art college, or treeless inner city slum (1998, p.43).

In other words, Social Constructivism concerns the individual's *knowledge about reality*, not the objective structures of reality itself (Patton 2002, p.96).

Choosing Social Constructivism as a theoretical paradigm has had several practical implications for this thesis, but two are perhaps most important. The first is that I have attempted to capture several different perceptions about reality, without trying to decide which is true, or truer. However, since I conducted the research among a study population who share the same world view, a *russified* one, their perceptions of reality are very similar. This allowed for cohesive data analysis and theory development. Yet, since Social Constructivism does not require the researcher to harmonize differences of perception, this paradigm helped me capture the details, nuance, and peculiarities that naturally occur in life, thus differentiating one person's experience from another's.

Second, a major tenet of Social Constructivism is that cultural and social phenomena can only be understood in context (Patton 2002, p. 96-98), something I was convinced of before I ever heard the term. Due to living and working cross-culturally for many years, I realized that attention to contextual factors—social, historical, religious, etc.—is critical to any study of human experience. This is why I have taken the time to thoroughly examine the religious historical context of post-Soviet Central Asia. I am convinced that Muslim conversions to Christ in this context are different than those taking place in other contexts, even other post-Colonial ones, because the local *islam* of the late Soviet and post-Soviet eras is significantly different from the local islams practiced elsewhere.

At the same time, conducting this study through the paradigm of Social Constructivism kept this study from becoming bogged down with *individual* religious experiences. Social Constructivism forces the researcher to balance the individual's construction of reality with the understanding that those meanings were generated through interaction with others in their social context, thus the final product is more like a collective picture than a collection of individual vignettes. This helps the researcher avoid idiosyncratic analysis and ensures the theories they developed are more likely to be useful beyond their exact study population.

3.2 Qualitative Research Approach

This study will be a strictly qualitative project based on the personal narratives of converts. Although quantitative and mixed methods have their place in the social science field, I believe the goals of this project were best served by a qualitative approach alone. Although quantitative studies are most helpful for understanding the breadth of phenomenon, that approach is less than desirable in this case for several reasons, two of which stand out. First, in order to conduct a quantitative study, the researcher usually needs some idea about the size of the total population from which they are drawing. However, since this is impossible with a socially deviant group such as converts to Christ in Muslim societies, even the best quantitative study would be suspect to some degree as to the test of representativeness. Second, quantitative survey instruments are by nature etic, that is they presuppose many things about the responses which will be given, and these presuppositions are part of the researcher's understanding, not the participants'. Since my stated aim is to discover the emic, or insider, understanding of conversion, a quantitative study seemed out of the question.

3.2.1 Analytical Approaches

In this subsection, I will explain the two methodologies that form the basis for my analysis of the interviews. The first is Grounded Theory (GT), and the second is Narrative Inquiry (NI). There are several reasons that I have selected to use a combination of Narrative Inquiry and Grounded Theory. One reason is that the originators of GT, Glaser and Strauss, considered Narrative Inquiry to be a good complement to their strategy (1967). Secondly, I believe both of these analytical methods fit nicely within my chosen research paradigm of Social Constructivism, since one of its fundamental tenants is that people construct their own version of reality. Narrative Inquiry provided a means by which I could gain a clear picture of that reality, while Grounded Theory helped to keep competing theories or explanations out of the way until a clear emic understanding had emerged. Now I should explore the meaning of Grounded Theory and Narrative Inquiry.

Grounded Theory

From the small library of books that have been written about Grounded Theory one might get the impression that GT is a complicated methodology taking many years to master. But nothing could be further from the truth. Grounded Theory is fundamentally two things; one, a commitment by the researcher to bring as few preconceived ideas to the data as possible; and two, the anticipation that plausible hypotheses will emerge from the data itself.

GT is not a methodology *per se*, but it is more properly understood as a way of thinking about and conceptualizing data (Strauss & Corbin 1998, p. 163). Grounded theories are generated by inductive logic, as the researcher speculates about how to explain relationships he is finding between concepts and ideas in the data set. As more and more examples arise that fit the researcher's speculations, he begins to generalize, looking for plausible explanations for what he sees. With the collection of more data and continued emersion in that set, these explanations firm in the researcher's mind, hypotheses emerge and notes begin to get longer and longer. These are the earliest conclusions and meaning-making interpretations appearing to the researcher, the eventual building blocks of theory, but they are as yet untested and unready for public view. Some of these early ideas eventually find enough support in the data that the researcher can formalize them into actual theory. That is *if* the researcher has robust critical thinking skills, a good data set, and is willing to spend significant time immersed in it.

However, the practice of Grounded Theory *does not* mean the researcher has absolutely no idea of what he might find. Rather, a GT approach means that whatever theories the researcher uses to explain the data will be substantially rooted in that data (Glaser 2003, Charmaz 2006). This is the "grounded" of Grounded Theory. Although the development of theory requires significant abstraction, in GT there must be a clearly traceable path back to the actual data. Since the data in which I will be "grounded" are personal narratives, this leads us to the second research approach that I have built this study upon, Narrative Inquiry.

Narrative Inquiry

The other approach to analysis I have employed is that of Narrative Inquiry. This research methodology has been defined by two of its best known theorists in the following way:

People shape their daily lives by stories of who they and others are and as they interpret their past in terms of these stories. Story, in the current idiom, is a portal through which a person enters the world and by which their experience of the world is interpreted and made personally meaningful. Narrative inquiry, the study of experience as story, then, is first and foremost a way of thinking about experience. Narrative inquiry as a methodology entails a view of the phenomenon. (Connelly & Clandinin, 2006, p. 375).

Narrative Inquiry is qualitative research *writ* large, and this is one of the reasons I like it. It demands that any ideas, theories, or findings proposed by the researcher truly be rooted in the actual statements of the study participants, words in context, not in our subjective interpretations. There are many reasons why I chose Narrative Inquiry. I will explore two in particular, the narrative turn in social sciences, and the issue of "reality" in religious conversion.

There has been a noted turn toward personal narratives as data, as the human sciences turned away from various Positivist modes of inquiry and meta-narrative approaches (Riessman 1993). Narrative Inquiry, also known as "Narratology" or "Narrative Analysis," emerged from Hermeneutic philosophy, which offers a perspective for interpreting texts—religious texts, newspaper articles, speeches by politicians, almost any form of communication that exists in written form. Hermeneutics facilitated the move in social sciences toward Narrative Inquiry by asserting that all attempts at meaning-making are interpretations rather than representations of independent reality (Patton 2003). The difference between any and all textual representations, and those that are properly called "narrative," is sequence and consequence. In narratives, "events are selected, organized, connected and evaluated as meaningful" by the storyteller, with the intention of using these choices to produce meaning (Riessman 1993, p.1).

Because Narrative Inquiry focuses on human experience, it has gained a wide usage in fields as diverse as literary theory, anthropology, theology, psychology and education—to name just a few. The main force of this narrative turn is the claim that humans are storytelling organisms; their lives are not only expressed in story, but are in fact shaped by the stories they tell (Connelly & Clandinin 1990). Or to take it a bit further, people are not simply characters in the stories they tell, rather their stories *are* their identity, one that is "created, told, revised and retold throughout life" (Lieblich, Tuval-Mashiach & Zilber 1998, p. 7). This is important to recognize because the opposite seems to have reigned in the past. As I previously noted, Daniel Varisco wrote an entire book, *Islam Obscured,* on the issue of Islam's being misrepresented because seldom, if ever, do researchers use the actual words of contemporary Muslims as data. Varisco argues that much ethnographic writing about Islamic peoples is filled with *researchers* telling about and interpreting what Muslims say or do, yet contain very little of what *Muslims* themselves actually say or do (2005). This problem is not isolated to studies about Muslims. David Yamane argues that the misrepresentation has been much more widespread; that researchers often attempt to explain the meaning of this or that religious experience without documenting so much as a single word spoken by any person with that experience (2000). The result is that in the past scholars often produced theory which was not so much derived from those they studied as it was from the researcher's own perceptions of them. By committing myself to Narrative Inquiry, I have produced findings and theories that are more rooted in the actual words and meaning constructions of study participants than in my observations and ideas.

A second reason for using Narrative Inquiry is that it helps us overcome one of the great problems of researching religious experience—such experiences do not take place in the same realm as do natural phenomena. This obviously poses severe problems for those wishing to conduct empirical research. Just how does one examine the "reality" of something that has neither mass nor shape? The first step to overcoming this vexing problem is for the researcher to recognize that he cannot study the physical, mental and emotional dimensions of religious experience in real time—as if conducting a lab experiment. However, that does not mean religious experiences cannot be studied at all. David Yamane (2000) argues that although the experience itself is not accessible, its linguistic representations are. So while religious conversion may not be accessible through a phenomenological lens, we can explore narratives about it; and by doing so learn that experience is meaningful to converts. Jeppe Jensen takes this idea a step further and suggests that the only reason religious experience is accessible *at all* is because it is at one level a "semantic phenomenon" (2003, p. 305). The spiritual verities that believers profess to experience, or hope to in the afterlife, are simply beyond the reach of systematic, scientific inquiry. Therefore when studying religious phenomena, it is critical to demarcate between the experience itself and the linguistic representations of the same. If the researcher is not careful to do so, he will tend toward one of two mistakes. On the one hand, he may attempt to apply logic and rationality to "other worldly" entities and experiences, a scientific dead-end. Or conversely, he sometimes assumes that all things related to religious experience are just as inaccessible as the spiritual "realities" he proposes to express, and therefore avoids the topic altogether.

Thus a narrative approach to understanding conversion is warranted, even required, because religious reality is an inherently narrative construction. Whether it is a Native American shaman passing along their stories to the tribal youth, or the first century Christian evangelists dictating their memoirs of Jesus, the religious world is more narrative than it is tangible. While some would argue this is true for all of life, this is particularly so in the realm of religion because religious experiences do not exist in the physical sphere, only in constructions of shared reality—and that reality is shared through words. However, narrative, unlike the intangible nature of religion, does not impede thoroughly scientific study because "narrativity is the fundamental condition for the human and social sciences" (Jensen 2003, pg. 452).

3.2.2 Research sample

Gaining access to the stories of Muslim converts to Christ had certain difficulties, namely that of identifying converts, and gaining the confidence required for them to share their stories. They are a classic example of a "hidden population," a study population that is "a subset of the general population whose membership is not readily distinguished or enumerated based on existing knowledge and/or sampling capabilities" (Wiebel 1990, p.6). Therefore, I have used a sampling strategy that is common for hidden populations, *network sampling*. This method of sample selection begins by interviewing a few well-situated people, or insiders, and then asking them to refer the researcher to others who they believe will have "information rich stories to tell" (Patton 2003, p. 230).

As a result of my previously living in Central Asia, I began the research process with connections to several Muslim converts to Christ, many of whom were willing to both give interviews and help me identify others for the same. Whenever possible I asked for a referral from those that I interviewed, thus forming a "chain" of informants which moved away from immediate relationship with myself and spread my sampling wider into the general population. Lee has pointed out that the use of personal connections in this way can be a major advantage when dealing with highly stigmatized populations because the process works as a referral system. Such intermediaries vouch for the researcher's *bona fides* when they make recommendations, which in turn encourages new people to participate in the study, and critically, to participate without reserve (1993, p.67).

This approach to sampling would be deficient in a quantitative project because it does not derive its validity from statistical probability theory. However, in qualitative research, this is actually a strength. Rather than simply enumerating large numbers of cases which might be very hard to properly analyze at depth, network sampling allows the researcher to focus on information-rich cases which they can reasonably expect to learn the most from (Abdul-Quader et. al. 2006). This is based on the premise that peers, in this case Muslim converts to Christ, are better able to locate and recruit other members of a hidden population *who have something worthwhile to say*. Also, as the name implies, network sampling takes advantage of the social networks in which the study participants are embedded. By drawing participants who are socially connected, the researcher is more likely to see true, socially constructed realities they share, rather than an artificial one that he constructs from socially disconnected people. Finally, in dealing with deviant or highly stigmatized populations, such as is the case in my research, network sampling is often the only way of gathering a sample, and as such must be used while dealing honestly with its limitations (Lee 1993, p.68).

In the end, this approach to sampling produced a data set of thirty-six interviews, gathered over the course of four trips to Central Asia in 2012 and 2013. As the chart below shows, the majority of these were conducted in Russian[41]; and they were recorded and later translated and transcribed into English for thorough analysis. However, on occasion, the ideas or topics from a recorded interview resurfaced in later conversation with that same person, at a moment when it was inappropriate or impossible to use the voice recorder. In such cases, these additions to the interviews were reconstructed as soon as possible from field notes, and then appended it to the interview transcript and noted as such.

Interviews were conducted until I recognized "sufficient redundancy" in the responses, i.e. a point was reached when the patterns of response began to repeat themselves and generate little or no new information (Schenul and LeCompte 1999). This fits well with Michael Patton's view of sample size:

> There are no rules for sample size in qualitative inquiry. Sample size depends on what you want to know, the purpose of the inquiry, what's at stake, what will be useful, and will have credibility, and what can be done with available time and resources (2002: 184).

A final note, since the sampling structure of this study relied on referrals from known converts, it was prudent to track the relational distance between myself and those interviewed. In the chart below, "relational distance" is a measure of this referral structure. Level 1 represents a person whom I already knew and could approach to request an interview. Level 2 are those

---

[41] Five interviews were conducted in English at the request of the participant.

referred to me by another, and Level 3 represents a further step away, a referral from a level 2 source. The primary reason for tracking this was to learn to what degree the referral system was successful.

Below is a table of the participants:

	Code	Age	Family Status	Language of interview	Relational distance	Approx. years since conversion
1	101F[42]	Mid 30s	Single	English	1	15
2	102M	Mid-30s	Married w/children	English	1	10+
3	103M	50+	Married w/children	Russian	2	15
4	201M	36	Married w/children	English	2	15
5	202F	Mid-20s	Married w/children	Russian	3	5
6	203M	42	Married w/children	Russian	3	20
7	204M	40s	Married w/children	Russian	3	15
8	205M	40s	Married w/children	Russian	3	10
9	206M	50s	Married w/children	Russian	3	15+
10	207M	Mid-30s	Married w/children	Russian	3	10

[42] The endings 'F' or 'M' on codes denotes female or male.

11	208M	50s	Married w/children	Russian	3	15+
12	301F	30s	Married w/children	Russian	1	10
13	302F	50s	Married w/children	Russian	1	15
14	303M	40s	Married w/children	Russian	3	15
15	304M	40s	Married w/children	Russian	1	15
16	305M	60s	Married w/children	Russian	3	15
17	306M	40s	Married w/children	English	1	20+
18	401M	70s	Married w/children	Russian	1	15
19	402F	50s	Married w/children	Russian	2	10
20	403F	30s	Married w/children	Russian	1	10
21	404F	60s	Married w/children	Russian	2	10
22	405F	30s	Single	English	1	15
23	406M	55	Married w/children	Russian	1	15
24	407F	40s	Married w/children	Russian	2	Unknown
25	408M	30s	Married w/children	Russian	2	10

26	409M	50s	Married w/children	Russian	2	10
27	410F	30s	Married w/children	Russian	2	-10
28	411M	50s	Married w/children	Russian	2	10
29	412F	30s	Single	Russian	2	Unknown
30	413F	30s	Married w/children	Russian	2	Unknown
31	414M	40s	Married w/children	Russian	2	10
32	415F	30s	Married w/children	Russian	1	Unknown
33	416M	40s	Married w/children	Russian	2	15
34	418M	20s	Single	Russian	3	5+
35	419M	30s	Married w/children	Russian	2	10
36	420M	57	Married w/children	Russian	1	15+

As can be seen from the data above, all but two of the participants had already been believers in Christ for approximately ten or more years at the time of their interview. It seemed that my local informants were only willing for older, more established believers to be exposed to the research process.

3.2.3. Data Collection Methods

Data collection for this study consisted of semi-structured interviews with open-ended questions. However, before continuing, I should explore what I mean by a semi-structured interview, and the implications of that for this study.

The term *semi-structured* interview conjures up images of something generic, perhaps a standardized set of house plans—a certain degree of variability for individual taste—but otherwise much the same. The structure, or framing, of the house is clear and set in advance. The idea of *structure*, however you understand the prefix *semi-* modifying it, is the defining characteristic of this kind of interview. Then there is the issue of *open-ended* questions. This concept, too, is problematic. An *open-ended* question sounds like a conversational *cul de sac* from which escape is possible, but not probable. It seems to me that both of these terms define a certain type of interview by what it is not - a survey, rather than by what it is - a chance for the study participant to tell their story. So while *semi-structured interview* is technically accurate in this case, there needs to be a better way to describe the kind of interviews which yielded the data for this study.

To begin with, I conceived of my interaction with participants more as conversations than as interviews. Not only that, I deliberately kept them as very one-sided conversations for reasons that will be clear shortly. The differences between a *conversation* and an *interview* are numerous. For example, interviews have built-in perceptions of power. The structure implies that the interviewer is in control as he asks questions, and the interviewee submits to that power by answering specifically the questions asked. On the other hand, conversations are two-way streets;

both parties have control over the direction they take. Police officers and potential employers interview people, friends have conversations. Furthermore, subliminal messages of control and power are problematic in any research setting, but they can be lethal in cross-cultural research. If the study participants sense power in play, it usually produces one of two outcomes. One, they will tell the researcher what they think he wants to hear; a common response in contexts of authoritarian governments like those of post-Soviet Central Asia. Or, the participants may chaff at the indignity of feeling controlled by the foreigner, which of course quickly destroys any rapport between researcher and participants.

Another important distinction between *interviews* and *conversations* is that when someone's responses range widely in an interview, we consider that he is "off topic," and the interviewer must return him to the task at hand. Conversely, in a conversation, much more latitude is normal, and there are often ribbons of thought that move toward seemingly disparate subjects. This latitude is critical if the researcher is looking for an emic perspective on a phenomenon. There is extensive evidence from cognitive science that human memory is not random, but organized; and this mental structure is best revealed in free recall. "When an individual is asked to recall a story, a picture, a word list, or any event at all, the parts of elements of that event tend to be reorganized in the individual's report. Cognitive research has shown that elements of events which are grouped together in recall can be assumed to be linked somehow in that individual's mental structure" (Freeman, Romney, and Freeman 1987, pg. 313). Thus, the participant's own structure of thought and perception is best revealed when the interviewer's own are the least intrusive, i.e. the interviews have the minimum structure possible while still furthering the larger aims of the research.

The challenge then becomes for the researcher to stay out of the way, so that the participant's emic perception can come through. And this is indeed a challenge. When a researcher is thoroughly grounded in his field of study and in his research context, it is quite common for him to *think* he more or less knows the direction an interview should go and what subtopics to expect. Thus the researcher develops a strong, though often unspoken, structure in his mind and he guides the interaction to make sure they cover all the important elements of that structure. This would make sense *if* the researcher were more knowledgeable than the participant on the topic of their conversation. But since we are talking about the study participants' own personal experience, surely they know more about it than the researcher does. And since we are looking for emic structures, participants must be the ones who control the direction of the conversation, to determine what is included and excluded, to ensure that all the important bases are covered.

This is an important methodological distinction to make. If we believe, and I do, that the converts know what is important, and what is not, in the story of their conversion, then we should gladly cede control over the direction of such interviews and allow participants to take the conversation in unexpected directions. This is how emic perspective is discovered. This is the seedbed from which grounded theory emerges.

Aside from personal problems with control, I think the reason many researchers are uneasy with this approach is that they have been trained to use structure to find what they are looking for in data, rather than uncovering the latent structure inherent in the data. The later approach, the one I have used, places less emphasis on research design and stresses the researcher's analytical skills. This approach offers space and freedom for participants to develop and articulate not just their thoughts, but *the structure of their thoughts*, rather than cutting their self-understanding into segments which neatly fit the researcher's preconceived structure which is reflected in the way they structure interviews. Thus, simply asking participants to tell their story, with a minimum of pre-planned structuring questions, allows insights not only into small segments of data, i.e. answers to questions, but it helps display the participant's own systems of meaning.

However, even as a minimalist, I acknowledge there needs to be some degree of structure to the research conversation, or we might never uncover anything of substance on the desired topic. Thus I did use a protocol, but it was very basic, consisting of three very open-ended questions and a few possible probes:

1. Describe the spiritual environment you grew up in.
    a. Who were the key spiritual people around you?
2. When and how did that change?
    a. Who was involved in this change?
    b. What were the main factors in this change?
    c. What was the first time you remember hearing about Jesus?
3. Tell me about your spiritual life today.

Of course this does not represent the sum total of my side of these conversations, but this was as far as my advance structuring went. Again, the goal was to ask questions that would start the conversation in the right direction, yet were open enough to facilitate meaning-making by the participant as they spoke. Ultimately I came to call these "framed conversations." By that, I mean conversations that were certainly not completely open-ended, but were "framed" by my interest in the participant's conversion. However, within in the width and breadth of that frame, there was virtually unlimited white space, room for the participants to tell their story, to include or exclude details as they would chose. In this way I tried to help each participant offer a narrative that is truly his own, yet one that would further the inquiry of this study.

3.2.4 Data Analysis Methods

There are many ways researchers can approach reading, interpreting and analyzing personal narratives as they make sense of them. In this study I have used two approaches—Holistic-Content and Categorical-Content analysis. The first of the two, the Holistic-Content approach, has the goal of finding a holistic or global impression of the narrative that harmonizes the narrative whole with its various parts. This is accomplished by the researcher reading the material several times, paying special attention to larger, thematic elements, or elements that might be possible building blocks of emerging themes. This broad perspective is then supported by a specific section of the narrative, a subtext that represents the whole. This type of analysis requires the researcher to have a firm grasp of each participant's story, something only gained through repeated, careful and empathetic readings (Butler-Kisber et al 2003, pp. 139-142). This is not an approach for those who are in a hurry or who want "hard edges" and lots of numbers about their data. One drawback to the Holistic-Content approach is that it requires narratives with strong, cohesive themes, which is not always the case. Therefore, I have chosen to also use a second, complementary approach which is more applicable to "segmented" stories—narratives that touch on multiple themes.

Miles and Huberman point out that qualitative researchers are often faced with a tension between the particular and the universal; to somehow reconcile the uniqueness of the individual case with the need for a more generalizable understanding of the processes they observe in the data (1994, pg. 173). For this I have chosen to use Categorical-Content. In contrast to the "big picture" reading of Holistic-Content analysis, Categorical-Content begins by breaking-up the narrative into relatively smaller units of content based on emergent themes[43]. After identifying portions of subtext that are particularly relevant, the researcher categorizes them by thematic concerns, then conducts analysis from the perspective of these themes rather than whole interviews (Lieblich, Tuval-Machiach, and Zilber 1998, pp.112-114). These themes are then developed using the material contained in subtexts from different interviews. There are many different types of analysis that can be used on these subtexts. I have focused on descriptive analysis as being more compatible with the Categorical-Content approach. Thus, Categorical-Content analysis allows the researcher to develop a thorough interpenetration of ideas between various interviews in the data set, again, a nice complement to the "individual stories" of Holistic–Content analysis.

While these two approaches are different in significant ways, they share a focus on narrative content, thus are complementary. And since both deal with content, both require some

---

[43] Here I refer to themes as "emergent" because I have conducted analysis within a Grounded Theory framework. Narrative researchers can and do sometimes use predetermined themes in Categorical-Content analysis, depending on the research tradition they are working from.

means of labeling portions of text. The most widely used and adaptable method for this procedure is *coding*; therefore, it is to that and related analytical processes that I will now turn.

Coding is perhaps the most important analytical tool of a qualitative researcher. At its most fundamental level, coding a text is nothing more than assigning a name or symbol to groups of similar ideas or phenomena that the researcher notices in his data set (LeCompte and Schensul 1999, pg. 55). Because codes are attached to specific sections of the data, they primarily function at the level of description, giving textual content to the researcher's ideas. However, codes can also be considered the first step toward abstraction because they are later used to help identify patterns and themes in the data. In keeping with my overall Grounded Theory approach, the codes I used were all inductive; that is, they were suggested by reading the data itself. None were predetermined. Through a repetitive cycle of reading, analyzing, and then rereading narratives, some codes were discarded, others changed names, and several were merged. This activity is part of the constant comparing and modifying that is a hallmark of Grounded Theory research (Glaser 2003).

At the same time as I read and coded interviews, I practiced what is often called "memoning[44]." These memos are short notes that are attached to sections of the text, which serve several functions. One of the fathers of Grounded Theory gave what is still the classic definition of a memo in this approach to research, "[A memo is] the theorizing write-up of ideas about codes and their relationships as they strike the analyst while coding… it can be a complete sentence, a paragraph, or a few pages…it exhausts the analyst's momentary ideation based on

---

[44] Various analytical processes such as coding and memoing were facilitated by the use of ATLAS.ti research software, version 5.2.21© 1993-2008, byATLAS.ti Scientific Software Development GmbH, Berlin. www.atlasti.com.

data with perhaps a little conceptual elaboration" (Glaser 1978, cited in Miles & Huberman 1994, pg. 72). Therefore, we can say that memos are primarily conceptual in nature as they tie together various concrete data units (codes). However, my use of memos went far beyond this. They also served as vehicles for thinking and exploring ideas through the process of writing process, thus facilitating the capture of new insights as they emerge. One of the advantages of using textual memos is that like codes, they anchor the researcher's thoughts to the actual words of participants, thus capitalizing on one of the strengths of Grounded Theory.

At first glance, coding and memoing seem like little more than technical procedures performed on a text, but they are much more. Miles and Huberman call then part of the "ladder of abstraction" which moves the researcher from description to explanation by slowly shifting the thought process from first, descriptive, to thematic, to patterning, and finally to developing mental "frameworks" (1994, pg. 91). Several of my own text memos became, for all practical purposes, the first drafts of some of the analysis presented in Chapter 4.

3.3 Ethical Considerations

Researchers in both the physical and social sciences have to carefully consider ethical concerns in their work. While a Narrative Inquiry research project has a lower potential for harm than, say, clinical trials for a new vaccine, there are always ethical considerations whenever human subjects are involved as subjects of a research project. However, this superficial commonality does not mean that the ethical constructions from one domain of science should be indiscriminately applied to the other. This is often a problem for social science researchers because the commonly held standards of ethical conduct were developed to address needs in the physical sciences, and some of them are poorly equipped to address the realities of social science research. In order to form a robust, yet relevant ethical stance for this research, I considered two fundamental ethical issues, the "risk-benefit equation" and principal of "informed consent."

The risk-benefit equation comes to us primarily from the field of medical research. It asks, "Do the risks to the participants compare to the potential benefits of the study?" The problem of applying this to social sciences research is the "ad hoc character of qualitative research makes calculating the risks and potential benefits of a project very difficult" (Larossa, Bennett, and Gelles 1981, 304-305). In fact, some researchers have argued that the ideas of harm and benefit are irrelevant in the context of ethnographic fieldwork because harm is rarely quantifiable, and benefit is difficult to identify (Cassell 1980, pg. 35). As it concerns this study, the risks to participants are not irrelevant, but they are indeed hard to quantify. The upside is that the participants themselves understood the risk of talking to me far better than I could have.

The second fundamental concern is that of *informed consent*, something which has been called the cornerstone of the ethical behavior and concern for the welfare of research participants. Unlike the "risk-benefit equation," informed consent is not difficult to practice and should be a basic ethical habit that researchers must cultivate as part of their respect for those participating in their study. At its core, informed consent means researchers are open and honest about the nature of the research project, offering participants sufficient information for them to make an informed decision about their participation (Larossa, Bennett, and Gelles 1981). Of course this presupposes that a reasonably healthy relationship exists between researcher and participant for the duration of their interaction.

With these things in mind, I found the best way to maintain a clear ethical footing in my fieldwork was to focus on informed consent based on an open, healthy relationship with study participants. I encouraged participants to evaluate the risks through interaction with me, and by consulting other participants. Together, we negotiated issues such as who would and would not participate, how I would handle their stories, and data security. Not only did this contribute to the level of transparency participants offered me, it also made for ethical parameters that were meaningful. I contend that focusing on ethics from a relational perspective is a better choice than the more legalistic approach taken by some universities which use lengthy "informed consent" forms. I am thankful that the University of South Africa allowed me this course of action.

3.4 Reliability and Validity

There has always been debate as to how social scientists should evaluate the quality of their findings. Many terms have been used: *rigor, validity, transferability, reliability,* and *trustworthiness,* to name a few. I chose to focus on two of these, *reliability* and *validity.* The first of these, reliability, concerns accuracy and faithfulness with regards to another referent. As such, I suggest that in a Narrative Inquiry project, reliability is best understood as fidelity to the words and thoughts of the participants. Did the researcher capture accurate accounts? Are the findings rooted in the actual words of participants? Thus, narrative inquiry that demonstrates a close and clear connection between the words of participants and the inferences drawn by the researcher has demonstrated that it is reliable. In the case of this research, one way I built reliability into the heart of the project was by taping of all interviews and then producing word-for-word transcriptions for analysis. Although many ethnographers rely on conversation notes rather than recordings, in the case of Narrative Inquiry, I reasoned that reliability would suffer without accurate verbatim records of participant's actual words, particularly given the nature of bilingual communication[45]. In other words, in this study, reliability is a function of the rootedness of the data, and every effort has been made to accomplish that. Nevertheless, data is only the basis for research findings, not the findings themselves; therefore, we need a second construction, *validity*.

Validity is a critically important concept, the boundary line between what is acceptable and unacceptable in qualitative research. It is generally understood as "the trustworthiness of inferences drawn from data" (Freeman et al 2007, pp. 26-27). Consequently, the qualitative researcher must demonstrate through the way he handles the data why others should trust his findings. However, it is important to note that validity is about "*inferences* drawn from data" (*ibid*). Thus validity involves imprecise mental operations such as reasoning, interpretation, even conjecture, all these being synonyms of "inference." This being the case, we do well to remember that social science research concerns human meaning-making, and as such, it has very little to do with the numerical exactitude of physics or chemistry. Polkinghorne has suggested that rather than being driven by mathematical certainty, social scientists need to aim to produce results that are believable (1998, p. 160).

---

[45] See section 3.3.1 on data collection methods.

To summarize, since this study falls within the research paradigm of Social Constructivism, which emphasizes the socially generated nature of reality, reliability is more closely related to fidelity to the words and thoughts of the participants than to externally existing constructions that need empirical verification (Bruner 1991). Therefore, my goal was not to produce findings that could "prove" certain theories, rather I have striven to produce findings that are reasonable. I have aimed for a kind of reliability and validity that are rooted in the data itself, yet which stand up to the academic rigor by clearly falling within the milieu of relevant social science thinking.

3.5 Limitations of Study

By its nature, social research has certain limitations. In the case of qualitative studies like this one, there is one particular limitation that I will briefly account for now, that is the generalizability of the findings. One of the great values of qualitative research is the depth of description it can produce, but that necessitates smaller sample sizes, thus limiting the degree to which a study's findings can be generalized. Also, since my sampling plan was not based on statistical probability theory, it would be irresponsible to paint these findings as *representative*. Since this study is rooted in Social Constructivism, it is better to think of the findings in terms of descriptive exemplars, or illustrations, of how some *russified* Muslims have understood their conversion. However, since the findings were generated by Grounded Theory, it would be relatively easy for someone in the future to design a hypothesis-testing study to validate and enlarge on the theories generated here.

3.6 Summary of Methodology

This qualitative study is rooted in the theoretical paradigm of Social Constructivism. This challenges the traditional ontology of empirical science, that there is a single reality existing independent of any observer's perspective, with an ontology that asserts multiple, socially constructed realities through which people perceive their world. This is sometimes referred to as the emic, or insider perspective. We should note that socially constructed realities are not necessarily ontological realities because they are not always objectively true. However, while this is an important academic distinction, in the study of human experience, it makes little difference. The way people perceive their world is, to them, reality, or at least this is the contention of Social Constructivism.

In order to gain access to this socially constructed reality about conversion, I followed two complementary research approaches, Narrative Inquiry (NI) and Grounded Theory (GT). Narrative Inquiry is a hand-in-glove fit for Social Constructivism because it maintains that people both shape who they are and interprets their past by means of the stories they tell, and those narratives are a portal through which the researcher can enter that reality with them. This is particularly true of religious experiences such as conversion, which are inherently inaccessible except through their retelling. As for Grounded Theory, while it is often referred to as a research method, it is fundamentally a commitment by the researcher to bring as little preconceived theory to the data as possible. It is founded on the belief that plausible explanations and hypothesis will emerge from the data itself. The combination of Narrative Inquiry and Grounded

Theory gives the researcher maximum latitude in his pursuit of truly emic understandings of the phenomenon being studied.

Muslim converts to Christ are a classic example of a hidden and socially deviant population, thus I employed a sampling strategy appropriate for such a population, "network sampling." This method begins by interviewing a few well-situated insiders and then asking them to refer the researcher to others, thus forming a "chain" of participants which moves away from immediate relationship with the research, and spreads the sampling wider in the general population. Besides the practical benefits, this process is particularly helpful with highly stigmatized populations because the referrals help to establish the researcher's *bona fides*. This network approach to sampling produced a total of thirty-six usable interviews, gathered at various locations across Central Asia[46]. The majority of these were in Russian, which were later translated and transcribed into English for analysis. This data was gathered through what I have called "framed conversations." By this I mean conversations that were framed by my research interests, but with virtually unlimited space for the participant to tell their story as they saw fit. By conducting the interviews with a minimum of imposed structure, I allowed the participants to develop their own structure to the narrative, thus helping to further tease out the emic perspective.

The analysis of the interviews was conducted along the lines of two methods—Holistic-Content and Categorical-Content analysis. The first of the two is concerned with finding a global impression of a narrative, and then harmonizing the narrative whole with its various parts. It

---

[46] For the geographic parameters of the sample, please refer to the section on Geographic Context, pg. 4.

seeks meaning that is contained in a single narrative. However, this approach requires narratives with strong, cohesive themes, which naturally is not always the case; therefore, I chose complementary approach to also use, which is more applicable to "segmented" narratives, Categorical-Content analysis. In this schema, narratives are broken-up into relatively smaller units of content based on themes. The researcher then uses these thematic subtexts to conduct analysis that cuts across several interviews. Thus, by using these two forms of content analysis, the researcher can handle a variety of kinds of interviews, gaining different perspectives from each approach.

In light of the methods and procedures summarized above, I have every confidence that the findings of this study will be found to meet all expectations of academic rigor.

Chapter 4 – Findings and Analysis Related to *Russification*

4.1. A More Grounded Picture of *Russification*

We noted before that anthropologist Diane Austin-Broos said that conversion was "a form of passage, a turning from and to..." (2003, pg.1). As a major part of this thesis, in the introduction we dealt extensively with the matter of context, that is the nature of the Central Asian local *islam* which participants in this study are "turning from." Nevertheless, a brief summary is in order as we enter data analsys. By the end of the Soviet era, for the vast majority of the indigenous population in Central Asia, being a Muslim had very little to do with classic, essentialist Islam. Being Muslim meant for them being part of a community that is Muslim, not individual knowledge of sacred material or even regular practice of Islamic rituals. Not only this, but after 70 years of Soviet rule, Central Asian Muslims had reached a comfortable détente by simultaneously inhabiting two very different cultural spaces, Russian and Islamic. This produced a new meta- identity, something the literature generally refers to as *russified* Muslims.

However, as the analysis of interviews unfolded, I realized the picture above was incomplete and somewhat inaccurate. I will start with a few excerpts as I refine the model of *Russification* offered in my introduction:

> "There are different types of Islam, you know. Some are very fundamentalist, they pray 5 times a day, etc. some wear special dresses, but some believe themselves to be Muslims but they do not observe anything. They are nominal Muslims. Here in we have a nominal Islam, mixed with traditions. Central Asia

was not Islamic before, but when Islam came, it was mixed with traditions. And that's the Islam we still have… here our Islam is very Central Asian. It's like you asked me, if I knew the Koran, I didn't. Do I know Arabic to be able to read the Quran? No, I don't. 90% of people in Central Asia do not speak Arabic. They might have learnt some verses in Arabic but they do not understand the meaning." (206M)

Or:

"Of course, my parents were Muslims, but at the same time they were not. Because there was communism and my father was a communist, he was a party member, as well as his brothers, even until now they think of themselves as communists and party members. Of course at that time nobody even said the word 'God'. There was no mosque in our village… We were communists, nothing about God." (414M)

And here a woman's point of view:

"Yes, we are also proud. Everyone thinks of himself as a Muslim, even though they don't do any of Islamic rituals, etc. But if any of us becomes a believer [in Christ], they start screaming, 'Why did they do that? They are Muslims!' Even though they themselves do not pray five times a day or follow anything else. They don't even know the translation of the word Muslim." (410F)

And one more:

"Our parents were traditional Muslims, like everyone else where we lived. They observed only traditional holidays like *Kurban-ayt*[47], etc… But since we were little we were always told that there is God; that there will be the end of the world, but we didn't really have a lot of religious education but our parents always emphasized that God can see everything. They used phrases like *'Huda*

---

[47] This is the colloquial version of the formal Arabic term *'Id al-Kurban*, "the festival of sacrifice."

> *shukur'* ('Praise God' in the Uyghur language), etc. If someone did something wrong and everyone knew that, they didn't say that God will punish them, but they would say 'God's rope is long', which meant that the person does bad things but one day God will pull the rope." (406M)

Although I agree with Khalid that Central Asian *islam* is not primarily about individual knowledge of sacred material or even regular practice of Islamic rituals (2007), that does not mean that no one in the region is actually a practicing Muslim. Several of the participants reported growing up in families that were practicing:

> "When I was growing up, there were my parents and four children in my family. We were growing up thinking of ourselves as Muslims. Not just our ancestors, but my father was practicing *namaz*[48] prayer, he made my mother read *namaz* and wear *hijab*. He was searching for God. My mother read *namaz* and they both told me that when I will turn 12, I will also read namaz and wear hijab." (202F)

Or on a more personal level:

> "I was trying to be a good Muslim. I would try to pray 5 times a day, but I was working in the bazaar so I could only pray before and after work. I asked one old grandmother about this and she said, 'don't worry, one can only do what they can do, and that is enough.' But I kept the fast, you know the Rosa, 3 years in a row. I fasted all 30 days." (408F)

So we can see that the effects of Russian influence on the Muslim population were uneven. One further, quite striking, example of this is to look at two very different reactions, both by post-Soviet Muslims of about the same age, when their daughters converted to Christ:

---

[48] *Namaz* is used in Turkic languages as the equivalent of the Arabic *Salat*, meaning ritual prayers. It is probably derived from a word for "the place of prayers" (Burton-Page 1993, p. 947).

"But when my mom saw the Bible, on my table, when I said I'm going to the church, she said, 'I'm going to burn in hell because of you, because you changed our religion"... She beat me, she threw out me from our house. It was a difficult time." (405F)

And now from a father, reflecting on his daughter's conversion which happened some months preceding his:

"At that time I was divorced officially with my wife and my wife went to Russia to do business and I would stay home to watch our daughter. At that time I had a Russian girl-friend and she was telling me, 'How come your daughter reads the Bible? You are Muslims, aren't you?' I said, that's OK let her read it. I don't mind." (420M)

One parent is quite angry, rejecting her daughter's new faith claims (albeit temporarily) while the other was completely nonplussed. The first is something close to the stereotypical Muslim response we expect to a family member's conversion, the second surprisingly indifferent to say the least. Yet these responses typify a dichotomy that I saw in the study. Some converts in post-Soviet Central Asia faced verbal and physical abuse, while on the other end of the scale, others experience no significant interference from family. These vastly different responses illustrate that we are actually dealing with two different kinds of religious backgrounds, or at least that the religious contexts for different converts are different enough as to require greater granularity than calling both of these contexts *russified* Muslims.

Finding 1: As it concerns conversion to Christ, the impact of Russian culture on Central Asian Muslims is best thought of as a continuum, with *Russification* on one end and *Sovietization* at the other.

Soviet-era scholar Vernon Aspaturian argued that the phenomenon is better understood using two terms—*Sovietization* for the wider concept, and *Russification* to refer to a distinctly different and deeper phenomenon than *Sovietization*. He defines *Russification* as "the process whereby non-Russians are transformed objectively and psychologically into Russians, and is more an individual process than a collective one" and the *Sovietization* of Muslims as "the process of modernization and industrialization within the Marxist-Leninist norms of social, economic and political behavior" (1968, pg 159).

Originally, during the process of reviewing the literature, I rejected this view as too abstract because I could not see how it might be operationalized, i.e. how one might practically identify when and if someone had been objectively transformed into a Russian on a psychological level. However, I have revisited Aspaturian's idea because the data showed a way to operationalize the distinction by their effect on religious behaviors and beliefs. Therefore, I would argue that as it concerns religion, *Sovietized* Muslims are those who were enculturated into many aspects of Soviet community life and thought, but still maintain some degree of theological content as part of their identity as Muslims, even if that content is minimal. On the other hand, *russified* Muslims are those for whom their "Muslim" identity has been so totally transformed into an ethnic identity that it no longer have any meaningful religious content. These have so entered the Russian worldview that reading a Russian religious text (Bible), or believing in a Russian religious figure (*Yesus Christos*[49]), were acceptable possibilities; even to the point where one such *russified* man briefly joined the Russian Orthodox church. After many years of

---

[49] *Yesus Christos* is the Russian language version of "Jesus Christ."

hearing about Jesus and spiritual searching, this man began talking with a Russian Orthodox Christian at work:

> "I saw that one of my colleagues had an Orthodox book about apostles. So I asked him and he told me that Orthodox faith is the right faith. So that's where I went. But I would hide it from my family and my Mom because I was afraid of misunderstanding and conflicts. So I went there and was baptized in the Orthodox Church, with the cross. To me the most important thing was coming to Christ. I was not so sure about their laws at that time but that was not the most important for me at that time. There are a lot of Russian traditions in the Orthodox Church that confused me but Christ was the most important for me." (206M)

Although I now agree with Aspaturian's construction, using *Sovietization* as the term for the larger phenomenon, and *Russification* for one end of the spectrum, I do not wish to waste time arguing about nomenclature. Since the use of *Russification* is so entrenched I will keep with the common usage. However, it is important to realize that *Russification* covers a wide spectrum of cultural change, ranging from those who simply conformed to Soviet era social patterns (including the use of the Russian language), all the way to Muslims who became psychologically Russian, thus people with a truly hybrid identity.

For those on that end of the scale, with a hybrid identity fusing Russian and ethnic Muslim aspects, the Russian-side of the identity served to them a sense of belonging to a group larger than their tribal affiliation. In other words they had become part of the "new Soviet man." Therefore, becoming Christian only involved switching one meta-identity with another, Russian with Christian. The other half of their sense of self remained intact.

However, the spectrum of cultural changes we call *Russification* are only one of the mechanisms that facilitated Central Asian Muslims moving across the wide cultural chasm that separated them from Christianity. Another one that looms very important in the interviews has to do with the metaphysical location of Jesus/*Isa*.

4.2 Metaphysical Location of Jesus/*Isa*

In several of the conversion stories I have studied, the participant was not the only one converted, but the central figure of Christianity likewise undergoes a major transformation of his own. But first we need to locate Jesus in the traditional thinking of Central Asian Muslims:

> "I knew that he [Jesus] was one of our prophets, and I knew that he was like the Russian God. That is what all of us call Jesus, the Russian God. But I knew that he was really one of our prophets." (205M)

> "I thought, 'Jesus Christ and the Bible are not for me. It's for the Russians, it is not for Muslims… From what I understood, if I become a believer in Christ, I will go to heaven. I just couldn't understand one thing: I was born Uzbek[50], in a Muslim family, so can an Uzbek believe in Jesus Christ?" (203M)

Here is one man's initial response when his wife started believing in Christ:

> "I thought she was going to a Russian orthodox church and crosses herself over, that Jesus is Russian God, I thought, this is it. She also took our daughter there, I was against that! I said, 'You go but don't take our daughter there!' I really persecuted them; I hated them for that." (411M)

---

[50] Uzbeks are one of the Turkic nationalities that live in Central Asia. They are historically Muslim.

Simply put, Jesus was the Russian God, thus for a Muslim to believe in him was absurd, even if there later turned out to be something attractive about faith in him. At least at the beginning of that interest, it seems to have made a significant difference whether they understood him to be the *Yesus* of the Russian Baptist and Orthodox Churches or *Isa Masih*[51], located somewhere in the wider heterodox world of Islam. We see this very clearly in the story told by one young woman as she reflected on her first encounter with the Christian message when she took a friend to a Christian drug rehab program:

> "We went into the church while there was already a service. And there was one guy on the stage, and he was sharing his testimony. About himself, that in this building many years ago I killed one guy, and now God saved me and I am preaching in the same building. I remember, I thought this is really, this minister, these people, will really help to (*sic*) my friend. So but every Sunday we came and I thought Jesus was not my God, he is the god for Russians, for the European people." (405F)

The Christian message seemed powerful and attractive, but it was inaccessible because Jesus belonged to someone else, he was "the Russian god." Then her story continues as someone changed the "location" of Jesus:

> "Then this guy I met in the church, the first time I went in, he asked me 'do you believe in Jesus?' I said to him, no, how can I believe in him, I am Muslim…Then he started to say about Jesus that he is *Kurban*[52], that he died not only for Russians and other people, but for you yourself.

---

[51] *Isa Masih* is the Quranic term for Jesus the Messiah. Converts in Central Asia use the term with a thoroughly Christian meaning despite the fact that orthodox Islamic usage is very different and excludes and sense of deity.
[52] *Kurban* comes from Hebrew, via Arabic, meaning "Sacrificial victim" (Wensinck 1986, p. 437).

<u>Interviewer: Was that the first time anyone ever used any terms like *Kurban*, or anything like that? Before then it was always Russian religious terms?</u>

Yeah

<u>Interviewer: Did that make a big difference for you?</u>

Yes, of course! Of course because I thought he knows really. He became a little bit closer to me. He did not say Jesus, *Yesus* in Russian, but he said *Isa Masih*[53]. That was the first time. It touched me, really touched me." (405F)

Another participant explained why the use of Islamic terms made an emotional difference:

"Yes, I heard that Christ is '*Masih*' and I liked that there is a different way to pronounce it, instead of saying Christ. So even if I used those words, it sounded much better than Jesus Christ.

<u>Interviewer: So to you it made a big difference?</u>

Yes because it was a real stumbling block. I heard the name *Isa* from my grandfather who was a Muslim, he said that *Isa* was coming back to judge the world… because I heard about Isa before and perceived Him as 'our prophet,' it meant that I did not sell my faith and did not betray the faith of my fathers. So it was important for me to know that it is part of our traditional beliefs." (416M)

Because of the long Russian Orthodox presence in the region, Central Asian Muslims all grow up knowing that *Yesus Christos* belongs to the Russians, or we could say that he exists in

---

[53] *Isa* is the Arabic pronunciation of the name Jesus, and *Isa al Masih, Isa Masih,* or simply *Masih*, are the Turkified versions of the Arabic term for "Jesus the Messiah," i.e. *Yesus Christos* in Russian.

the Russian metaphysical world. But when *Yesus Christos* becomes the Muslim *Isa Masih*, he becomes accessible, vaguely Islamic, like someone written about in the Quran.

<u>Finding 2</u>: For many Central Asian Muslims Jesus is inaccessible until he, as *Isa*, enters into their culturally-constructed metaphysical landscape. The primary example of this linguistic phenomenon is the change of the Russian religions figure *Yesus Christos* into *Isa Masih.*

The importance of this change of metaphysical location is rooted in a couple of anthropological concepts. First, since conversion "to Christ" lies at the core of this thesis, we believe Roger was right when he wrote that religious conversion was perhaps best understood as "taking on a relationship with new supernatural beings" (2003, pp. 109-121). These might be saints, angels, demons, ancestors, and/or deties; but conversion means a person changes which of these beings they relate to. In our case, we might say that Mohammad (most likely in the role of saint) has been left aside and Isa (perhaps a cross between saint and deity) is adopted. Secondly, if conversion is about a new relationship with a different supernatural being, then the context or location of being is important. While this "location" is entirely metaphysical, and a cultural construction, Lambek reminds us that they are still "real, vivid, and significant to those who construct and inhabit them" (2002, pg. 2). Thus the cultural space in which a convert locates Jesus will carry emotional significance.

> "When you say 'Christian' to a non-believer, he thinks 'Orthodox' but when you say follower of *Masih* to them, they have a different understanding. Because the word *Masih* does not irritate their ear, like Russian words do, such as *Czerchov*[54],

---

[54] Russian word for church

Yesus Christos, etc. because they relate them to Russians. But when you say *Isa Masih* it sounds softer because it is in the Quran." (208M)

Another convert who is now an active evangelist among Muslims was clearly frustrated that his foreign Christian friends do not understand the importance of this issue as it relates to sharing the gospel with Central Asian Muslims:

"Anyway, Europeans [Russians and foreign missionaries] don't understand the difference between *Yesus* and *Isa*. They would ask 'why is it so important for you when you know that this is the same person?' So they were worried a bit, they were suspicious of this. They wanted us to leave that completely and they wanted us to be just like them. But deep inside I knew that this was not for me…I knew the barriers. I knew that only one letter or one word could hinder them [other Muslims] from coming and believing in Jesus. Of course to them, the Europeans, it was not important. Yet it is very important to us.

<u>Interviewer: So, for a Kazakh[55] who speaks fluent Russian, this is not the problem of a language but it is a problem of culture?</u>

Right. I myself was not a real Muslim, I never counted the *namaz*[56], was never committed, [and] because I studied in Russian, I had a more globalized thinking. But even despite that I was surprised because once I stepped into a European church; something began to wake up in me. So I realized that if it happens with me, who had nothing to do with Islam, what will happen to those who worship in Islam? The door will be closed to them. So I knew it was important to address that." (416M)

---

[55] Kazakhs are one of the Turkic nationalities that live in Central Asia. They are historically Muslim.
[56] "Counting *Namaz*" is the typical Central Asian way of referring to doing ritual prayers five times each day.

Also, it is not just Jesus who moves, but also other major Christian concepts. In the following interview we can see the central text of Christianity making the same move:

> "Then I was walking across the prison and I saw another man who had some brochures on a small table in his room. I went over to him and asked about these. They were spiritual books, and there was also a New Testament. This man was a Christian, I think he was Russian... he asked if I wanted to read the New Testament, and I said yes. It was in Russian. I read it quickly, I think I read the whole thing in one day... [My Russian friend] later he gave me a Uzbek *Injil*[57] to read. As I read the Uzbek *Injil* I understood more...as I read it I started to believe in *Isa* as the savior. I could see the way he did things and healed people and something in my heart was stirring. I started telling the other prisoners that they should believe in *Isa* because of all the wonderful things he did." (205M)

Also, the meetings that foreign missionaries organize on Sundays are Church, but gatherings of local Muslim converts are perhaps something else:

> "I kept wondering, why do people have to come to church? Nobody knows what you are really like at home or at work. We come, greet each other and go. No fellowship during the week. So I thought, this is not a *djama'at*[58], because a *djama'at* should be people in fellowship with one another. My neighbor is my *djama'at* because they see me, or my sister, that's what *djama'at* should be like. So I was wondering, why the Gospel should be only expressed by going to church?" (302F)

And another:

---

[57] *Injil* means "gospels" as in the message brought by the prophet *Isa*. However, many converts from Islam use the term to refer to the entire Christian New Testament.

[58] *Djama'at* comes from the Arabic root "to bring together, to unite" which expresses an ideal of the bond which unites individuals or groups (Zurayk 1991, p. 422). Turkic peoples in Central Asia often use the word to refer to a meeting with religious connotations. In the case of converts, it is often used in place of the Russian word *Czerkoff*, or church.

"We came to visit them [relatives who had converted] very often while in the capital city and she would talk with me and her husband would talk with my husband. My husband went to *djama'at* with them the very first Sunday. But I couldn't so I stayed home…Since we are Uyghurs, when we hear *Yesus Christos*, we think, this is a Russian God! So that was stopping me. When they were saying, *Khuda, Khuda*[59], I liked that. But whenever I heard *Yesus Christos*, I would shut down. They were thanking God for tea, for bread and cookies, and I really liked hearing it. All that was very appealing to me. Except when I heard *Yesus Christos*, then I ran away from them." (408F)

This moving of Christian ideas into the Islamic thought world extends even to the way converts pray over their meals:

"I usually say [to other Muslims] that I am a believer in *Isa Masih*. And I would openly say that I read the *Injil*. People would say behind me that I was a betrayer of Islam, a *Kafir*[60]…I used to tell people the term Christian, in the past, [but now] *Masahi* (a follower of *Isa Masih*)… I try to be careful in how I do things. For example, praying after the food not before. Praying in Islamic way, saying *Ameem* instead of Amen[61]… I purposefully choose not to do some things. Not to pray before food or by bowing my head.[62]" (201M)

---

[59] *Khuda* is the Uyghur word for God, as opposed to the more formally Islamic, and Arabic, *Allah*. This usage also probably points to the fact that the converts she is referring to were not previously regularly involved in Islamic worship rituals, thus the choice to use *Khuda* rather than *Allah*.
[60] Kafir originally meant an "ungrateful one," i.e. one who did not believe in the mission of Muhammad. In Turkic languages it eventually became a strong term of abuse which at times implies the one so being should be subject to the death penalty (Bjorkman 1990, pp. 407-409)
[61] This signifies the difference between the way Russians pronounce the word used as a common ending to prayers. Russians say *Amen*, and Muslims the same word, *Ameen*.
[62] Here he is referring to the differences seen in Central Asia between Christian meal-time prayers (bowing before) and Muslim practice of the same (looking up afterward).

Even though the linguistic transformation of Jesus might seem less significant to some, the larger complex of moving faith in him into Muslim cultural space always lurking around the edges:

> "Interviewer: Do you use the name *Isa* or *Yesus Christos*?
>
> You see, for me these two words are the same, because I have become a *russified*, so to me there is no need to 'translate' *Yesus Christos* into Uyghur[63] (his ethnic 'mother-tongue'[64]). All Russian-speaking Uyghurs do not have to 'translate' it. But Uyghur-speaking Uyghurs of course need to translate it into Uyghur. Most of people in our *djama'at* do that. But I didn't need to 'translate' the name of *Yesus Christos*; however, I did think that *Yesus Christos* was Russian. He had to do with the Russian church, with Christian religion, and Russians, not Uyghurs."(406M)

We can see that many related ideas moved with *Yesus Christos* from the Russian religious world into a new heterodox world of Islam; the central text of Christianity, the New Testament, is now transformed into the *Injil,* and Christian gatherings from churches to Djama'ats.

And finally, it is important to note that while there may have been several ways that this shift of metaphysical location took place, at least two came out clearly in the interviews. In some cases it was the result of a foreign missionary's teaching:

> "[The missionary] showed me which verses to read about Jesus. But I doubted that Quran said anything about *Yesus*, when *Yesus* was Russian? I was very confused. So when I began to read the Quran I discovered so many things! I was

---

[63] Uyghurs are one of the Turkic nationalities that live in Central Asia. They are historically Muslim.
[64] I have used this phrase for simplicity sake. It is beyond the scope of this thesis as to which language is properly considered the mother tongue of a *Russified* Muslim, Russian or their ethnic language.

so happy inside! I said, 'here it is! Muslims also believe in it! Why do they not tell us about *Isa* Who is it written for? If Muhammad didn't want us to know about *Isa*, he would not include him in the Quran and would say, believe in my only!' So I made a lot of discoveries. I developed deep love for God and for *Isa*. I began to study and now I wrote down all of the quotes about *Isa* from the Quran and the Bible." (402F)

Other times it was clearly the result of an indigenous thought process that had been informed by Quranic material:

"When I was little, my grandfather was a well-known mullah; where we lived everyone knew him and respected him. My grandfather had two wives. My father was supposed to also become a mullah. So he started counting the Namaz prayer. But before my grandfather died he said that the truth is in *Isa*.

Interviewer: He said that to your father?

Yes. He said, the truth is in Isa. My father wondered why he said that and he started studying the Quran. It was in 1997, I was 12. At that time my father started studying; he just got into a motorcycle accident and had to stay home for a while, so he had a lot of time to read. He read the Quran, what it said about *Isa* that He was born pure, that he healed the sick, raised from the dead and casted out demons. That's all that it says about Him. Oh, it also says that *Isa* will come back. So my father didn't understand anything from the Quran and he started studying the Bible. The Bible is very clear. So gradually he came to believe. At that time relatives came to our house and once they found out, they began to persecute him. They said, 'What will people say? Your father was a Muslim and so are we; why are you doing this?' They called him kafir. They said that he was paid to believe in Jesus. My father didn't pay attention. His older brothers even brought a mullah to him who told him, 'This is not true! Who told you this?' My father answered, 'Jesus is the Son of God. God sent Him to Earth'. He told that mullah, 'Open Sura

3, ayat 45 [in the Quran], and it says that *Isa* will come back in the end of the world. No man can come back like that, so I know this is the truth'." (418M)

So, whether it was the result of foreign missionary teaching, indigenous theological development, or likely a combination of the two, it is clear that a significant aspect of Muslim conversions to Christ in Central Asia has been the movement of Jesus from one metaphysical space to another. This move is demonstrated, and was perhaps even accomplished, by a shift in the choice of words used by those involved—convert and missionary alike. The central character of the Christian story was moved from being *Yesus Christos* of the Russians, to becoming *Isa Mesah* who by nature of his rootedness in the Quran, belongs to the cultural world of Muslims. Also, this points forward to our next major finding which has to do with the textularity of the faith being expressed.

4.3 A Textual Faith

Finding 3: A significant factor in the conversions of Central Asian Muslims is the legacy of Soviet era efforts to increase literacy. This laid the groundwork for the textual nature of Protestant Christianity which Muslims later encountered.

As we dealt with at length in the introduction, local *islam* in Central Asia had, for many years been marked by limited access to textual sources. This was not only because of Soviet sanctions against religion, but reaches much further back to problems with pre-Soviet literacy and clergical control of intellectual resources. Of course the Soviets helped to further remove Islam from its textual resources by closing madrasas and changing the script for indigenous languages from Arabic to Latin, thus severing people's connection with the wealth of Islamic writings from the past centuries. In the end, we reach a situation by the end of the Soviet era in which religious authority in Central Asia was almost exclusively based on tradition—and the textual sources of Islam had little day to day value. Although Islam is founded on a sacred text, in Central Asia this played a distant secondary role, if that much. Based on my interviews, it seems the average Muslim had very little contact with their sacred text. Here are a few typical responses:

"Interviewer: Did you read the Quran?

No, I only listened. Because Quran was read in Arabic, at that time we didn't have all the translations that are available now…. here our Islam is very Central Asian. It's like you asked me, if I knew the Quran, I didn't. Do I know Arabic to be able to read the Quran? No, I don't. 90% of people in Central Asia do not speak Arabic. They might have learnt some verses in Arabic but they do not understand the meaning." (206M)

"Well, my father was a member of the Soviet party, so my parents never were religious… they would only read Quran when someone died." (301F)

"We never read the Quran. I didn't even know that Quran is translated into different languages; I thought it was only available in Arabic. I didn't really think a lot about it." (302F)

> "I remember that my mom said that we [females] cannot read the Quran because only a pure person can touch the Quran. But a woman is dirty and cannot touch the Quran." (402F)

This lack of appreciation for sacred text runs completely counter to the high value that Soviet society put on literacy. Reaching all the way back to the earliest phases of the Bolshevik revolution, widespread literacy was a major social agenda in the Soviet Union (Clark 1995). Soviet authorities saw mass literacy as "the one clear channel for the deliberate and systematic inculcation of a set of [Soviet] values" and a means to move people away from the beliefs and values of their natal community (Darden and Grzymala-Busse 2006). Soviet authorities were certain that by introducing universal literacy they were bringing about the complete shift from the backward and outdated religion of the mullahs to an enlightened scientific materialistic worldview. Thus the hybrid-identity of *russified* Muslims caused an internal dilemma. Their Russian identity placed a significant value on knowledge and personal enrichment through reading, while their Muslim identity was completely walled off from this because of local tradition and a lack of Arabic language skills[65].

Yet in a way that would probably make Lenin roll over in his grave, this push toward a text-based authority helped lay the groundwork for later Christian missionary efforts among the Muslim population. Whether the conversion proponent was a local Russian Baptist or an Australian Charismatic, they were all Protestants, rooted in the theology of *sola scriptura*[66], therefore the faith they transmitted was highly textual. This is perhaps seen most clearly as a convert reflects on the two texts, the Bible and the Quran. This man was, by his own account,

---

[65] This includes a lack of local translations of the Quran.
[66] *Sola scriptura* is Latin for "by scripture alone," one of the rallying cries of the Protestant Reformation.

very secular and *russified,* but when his wife started attending a Christian meeting, something changed:

> "For whatever reason, it was when she became a Christian that Islam became very strong in me all of a sudden. I suddenly remembered that I was a Muslim. Despite the fact that I had a very secular life-style and was not acting like a Muslim… [So] I read [the Quran] in Russian, translated by Krachkovsky. But it was not clear. The Quran is not continuous and it is very hard to understand. Not a very clear language." (103M)

Here we see a very different reaction than the often cited Muslim love for the perfection of the Quran in Arabic. Either the text had lost something in translation, or just as likely, the process of *Russification* had so changed the reader that the literary esthetic of the Quran no longer spoke to his psyche. After more than ten years opposing his wife's faith in Christ he started reading the Bible:

> "I read it all the way through, because I loved its consistency and clear meaning. I didn't understand spiritual things at that time but I could understand the historical events. One of the books that really affected me was the book of Job. I am still not sure why exactly, maybe it was closer to my Muslim mentality, but for whatever reason even as a non-believer I read it many times. It is still one of my favorites." (103M)

We might say that the Soviet plan to use literacy, specifically in the Russian language, as a means of distancing Muslims from their natal religion worked, but it took unexpected turns once Soviet authorities controlled which texts were available. And if we are to consider strange twists, notice the counter-intuitive way that a desire to lead others to convert away *from* Islam was a catalyst for this *former* Muslims to start really engaging with the text of the Quran:

> "Some people say that Quran is like a bridge that you can use to invite people from Islam to Christianity. The problem is that many Muslims do not read the Quran so they lack understanding and they don't want to hear and understand... Even when I show them the verse in the Quran where it says that Allah will put *Isa* above all, and that salvation comes through Him, and Allah will punish people who do not believe in *Isa* and will not help them in the next life; there are even ayats that talk about *Isa*. I show these to them but even then they do not understand and do not accept... [I tell them] that there are also prophets in the Quran, like Moses, Abraham, etc. But it did not describe their story completely and there were some contradictions there. It said that Mohammad was the only prophet and I didn't like that. I already believed in *Isa* and thought of Him as my Lord but I then read the Quran so I could tell my parents that Quran also talks about Moses, David, and other prophets. I also told them that Mohammad was just a prophet but *Isa* was Lord and the Sacrifice of God. So I decided to hold on to *Isa* and to the Bible. I liked that it described the complete stories, and I liked the Gospel that talked about *Isa* being on earth doing good... Also, the epistles that clearly taught how we should live our lives because Quran does not teach that. <u>Right now I am also studying the Quran to use it to reach out to Muslims</u>." [emphasis mine] (304F)

This story adds another dimension to the way that *Russification* impacts conversion:

> "In 1994-1995-96 I went to Russia to do trading. <u>I was staying with my aunt who was Russian. I also stayed with my wife's sister, who was married to a Russian man</u>. They were telling me about Jesus and at first I said, 'No', as a Muslim. But I lived there for a month and God did a miracle. I went to church eventually and in December there was Christmas service and that's when I accepted Jesus Christ.

So we both [he and his wife] became believers in Russia. But even before that there were people who shared the Gospel with us. First time it was my coworker, she was Kazakh. But I did not accept that. Then two Russian girls came to our house and told us the Gospel but we did not accept it. <u>Then third time was when my wife's younger sister married a Russian man who was an assistant pastor, and she told us about Jesus.</u> We felt sorry for her, we thought, oh, she is so young and already lost! Then he came to visit us and shared the Gospel to us. Then fourth time we went to Russian and repented there, but God used 5 or 6 different instances to speak to us." [<u>emphasis</u> mine] (304M)

Clearly, the practice of Russian-Muslim intermarriage, one result of *Russification*, made subsequent conversions more likely. And it is worth noting that this effect is not just on those immediately involved, but on the Muslims who are part of the extended family as well.

And finally, no understanding of the textual nature of this new faith in central Asia would be complete without a look at the way Christian scripture impacted the development of this new convert's life. Below are the words of a 75 year old male, who converted in his 60s, was thoroughly *russified* and an avid reader who "could read a book over one night. I loved fiction and adventure." But after his conversion his attention turned the Bible, in particular he explains the nature of how the biblical text impacted him:

> "I accepted *Isa* in 1999, in June. It was a family summer camp… but was still very weak spiritually. But gradually I began to grow because I read the Bible every day. But when I read it first time I read it as fiction, not as a spiritual book… when we first came back home [from the camp], I read the Bible like a fiction. From creation to revelation. But I didn't understand anything of what I read. Over half a year I read the Bible three times. Cover to cover." (401M)

Later, when talking about his financial problems when he first converted:

> "When I read about Joseph, the son of Jacob, and the trials God put him through, I thought of my own trials. I said to God, 'You tested Joseph, and you are testing me. The time will come and you will bless me, too!' That gave me hope in God. I felt like I was Joseph, I was Abraham, so when I was reading those books I would put myself in their place.
>
> Interviewer: So you saw yourself in the Bible?
>
> Yes, I would put myself in place of Abraham.
>
> Interviewer: So the Bible story became your story?
>
> Yes, so in the church I raised the book and I said, this is the book about me. So each one of you take it as if it was written for you!" (401M)

This helps us see some of the contours of this "textual faith." As he read the Bible, he placed himself in the text, slowly rewriting his personal narrative as he read and reread its stories. This is exactly what Elizabeth Dufalt-Hunter recognized in her study of intercity converts to the Nations of Islam. Her thesis describes how the alternate the Nation of Islam offered African-American converts a completely new personal story in which they discarded a personal narrative of "bitches, whores and niggers" (p. 155) for a metanarrative in which black people were "once [a] great people—the source of all civilization" (p. 154). In the same way, the Bible offered this man a way to rewrite a personal narrative of failure—nominal Muslim faith and alcoholism—to become a man like the prophets of old. Quite a narrative transformation, and a story that could have easily been missed without the use of narrative inquiry in this study.

4.4 Agency

Whenever cultural change takes place, particularly when it involves a cross-cultural encounter, there is a question of agency. Who drives the change? Is someone driven by it? Who rightfully controls the verbs in the story? Sometimes these questions are clouded by general, socially reinforced impressions that we collectively hold for uncertain reasons. As it concerns the spread of Christianity, historian David Killingray argues that a "common view held by many people in the West is that Christianity was spread around the world by white missionary agents from the 'Northern' world." (2005). This perception has been given a gloss of negativity by many in academia, specifically anthropologists, since they often see foreign missionaries as their "enemies" because they believe that missionaries destroy culture (Stipe et al, 1980).

Now, onto this backdrop, paint the historic specifics of post-Soviet Central Asia such as the sudden geopolitical openness after the end of Communism. It becomes the inevitable conclusion that foreign missionaries were the vanguard of conversions among Muslims in the region. Or at least this is certainly what British anthropologist Mathijs Pelkmans would lead us to believe. In an article that smells of bias, Pelkmans speculates there are probably more than 1,000 foreign missionaries active among the five million local population of the little state of Kyrgyzstan. He furthermore leaves the impression that this is symptomatic of all post-Soviet Central Asia (2005, p. 884). If this impression is anything close to accurate, then we should find foreign missionaries to be the main characters in the stories told by Muslim converts to Christ in Central Asia.

However, although the logic seems right, the data does not support it. Of course, the caveat is that this study was qualitative, therefore it cannot produce "numbers" to correlate to, or contrast with, Pelkmans assertions. However, as we reasoned in the methodology section of this thesis, the fairly open, free recall methods of the interviews offer one of the best ways to capture study participants own perceptions. Thus from a qualitative perspective the issue is not how many foreign missionaries there are in Central Asia, but, *"Did study participants perceive foreigners as the primary agents of their personal spiritual change?"*

The best answer is, yes, but only occasionally. In only a few of the interviews did foreign missionaries play major roles. First we should look at a couple of interviews that do indeed support for the common perception of foreign missionaries being the primary agency of conversion:

> "One time one of our brothers got sick - he fell in the kindergarten and he injured his head. After that he had trouble sleeping at night, cried a lot from head-aches. We took him to doctors, did tests and check-ups but doctors could not determine what was wrong with him. But something was wrong. We took him to a therapist and psychologist but had no results - nobody knew what was wrong and what his diagnosis was... He was very young then; he would hit people, he could not recognize himself or us; it was hard. And what's interesting - it only happened at nights. During the day he was a normal child...
>
> At that time there was an American family in our neighborhood. They didn't tell us at that time but they were missionaries. They just moved to our neighborhood to live. They said they wanted to learn more about the culture, the people and the national system of these neighborhoods. So, my mother and we all became friends

with them. One day my mother could not take it anymore and she shared her problem with them…

They said to us, 'We will be praying for you'…Then later they invited us to their house to watch 'Jesus' movie. It was about the life of Jesus. We really enjoyed it. Several days later the wife came to us and this time she was sharing with us more openly. She said, 'Let me pray for this child for God to make him OK. It was in the evening. They prayed for our family and for my little brother and that night my brother slept all night through. He slept well and quietly till very morning. We were shocked; my Mom was shocked; she said, 'How is this possible? We tried everything - we took him to doctors, we read the Quran over him but all in vain. My mother ran to their house and asked, 'What did you do? What did you do to my son? He slept all night long! That's when they started telling us about Jesus. My mother believed right away…

They became very good friends; they had courses at our house every week on how to study the Bible and how to pray, and how to live a new life. I was watching all these things happen and I also enjoyed peace and quietness that came to our house. I also wanted to know more. I read children's books about Jesus." (202F)

Or an older man:

"Interviewer: When you accepted *Isa*, who were the key people that you talked about key spiritual things with?

I talked with leaders.

Interviewer: Locals or foreigners?

More with foreigners. Jim, Bill, Dan, I forgot a lot of names. I think there was Paul… Many people. There was also a woman in New Life [a Russian Charismatic church]. At that time, when I first came [to Christ], I talked more with foreigners, a lot of the spoke Uyghur and spoke Russian, so through them we would start small cell-groups, and organized tea-parties for believers, talking about the Word of God. That was a wonderful time and I am so thankful that He sent so many of His people from different countries - from America, Australia, etc.It was the will of God to bring the Word to Kazakhstan, and bring it to us, Uyghurs and Muslims here through foreign brothers. This is why I came to God." (401M)

While these first two excerpts come from narratives that very much support the view of foreign missionaries as primary agents of conversion, more often when participants mentioned them at all, foreign missionaries were in a secondary role, working with local Christians of various kinds:

"Interviewer: So at that time you were going to a Russian Baptist church, if I remember correctly?

Yeah,

So there were not any foreign missionaries, all local Christians?

When I was in the Baptist fellowship I was only single believer from a Muslim background.

So you were the only believer from a Muslim background in the church?

I didn't see them if they were there. I had the chance to meet with one German guy, missionary, who came to visit his relatives in that city and he mentioned, there was a Kyrgyz believer in a certain city. [He said I could] come and visit us and spend time with him, a couple days to spend among other believers. You know at that time I thought all Christians were Russians, I did not know that there were others like me. So I went to the city and spent a month there being among the first Christians among the Kyrgyz. I been there and just it was a real blessing time for me. These guys were really just inspired me, encouraged me, helped me to understand that I was not just one." (306M)

Notice how the foreign missionary's role was significant, but not as a primary agent of conversion, rather as a mediator between converts from similar Muslim backgrounds. In the following excerpt we can again see foreigners playing a significant role, but only several years after initial conversion and after the convert had been involve in a local church lead by of former Muslims themselves:

"Our older sister was first one to come to believe…it was in 1994. In 1995 she would take me to the capital city during school breaks. The church [she went to] met in their house and that's when I started going to church and read *Injil*. Of course we didn't tell our parents, our father didn't know about this for a long time… At first she went to a church, I think it is still around, it was called *Sevgi Mahallasi* ["neighborhood of love" in the Uzbek language].

Interviewer: Did you have a pastor? Was he local or a foreigner?

Yes. All of them were local. There was a woman; I don't know if she was a pastor or not… She is still there, she is local. I think she is Azeri… [But] I was young, I didn't understand it completely. So when my sister would take me there and I was in a home group, I didn't really understand what or why they were doing…I was 13 and I was simply too young to understand… When I moved to the capital in 2000 I started visiting other groups, too. Like there was a youth group called Halas - it's a Greek word - it was from Campus Crusade[67], there were foreign people from them who organized meetings [and] I went to some of the

---

[67] "Campus Crusade" is the name of an American Evangelical missionary group which focuses on college age young adults.

meetings… It was like a Bible study. So I went there to, and I was influenced by them as well. I began to understand things. Now I know who *Isa* is, now I know what He had done." (204M)

The above interview data helps us to articulate the next finding in this study:

Finding 4: The primary agents of Muslim conversions in Central Asia were usually local Russian Christians and other former Muslims turned evangelists. Foreign missionaries mostly played a secondary role, if any at all.

Now would be a good place to explore the kinds of local agency that did dominate the narratives, local Russian Christians and other former Muslims turned evangelists. First we will explore the agency of Russians.

4.4.1 Russian Agency

There were so many examples that it was hard to choose which interviews to draw excerpts from, but the ones below are characteristic of the larger phenomena:

> "Interviewer: When was the first time you heard about Jesus? How old were you?
>
> I heard about Jesus when I became 19 yrs. old, a friend of my father who worked with him, he shared with me about the NT and he shared about
>
> Interviewer: A local man?
>
> Yeah, he was a Russian guy working for my father [who] was the head of the shoe [manufacturing] company… So this guy shared with me about Jesus the first time when I was 18 years old and I got more... kind of it, was like a desire to know what was the meaning of this life. So I didn't know exactly how faith,

believing in Jesus, could transform a life. So until I really made a decision, it took like maybe two years, before I really made a decision… mostly [because] of the influence was this guy, from his sharing." (306M)

The next two women heard about Jesus when they were young, from Russian schoolmates:

"Interviewer: When is the first time you heard about Jesus? The very first time?"

I heard about Jesus when I was 8 years old, through one of my friends, she was going at that time to the Orthodox Church.

Interviewer: So she was Russian?

Yeah, she was Russian. And I remember she brought some book about Jesus, about him and his disciples. And I remember at that time I was really hungry for spiritual things. And I really wanted to know more about God because I was a Muslim, but this was really interesting…" (101F)

"I remembered that my Russian classmates also told me about Jesus, maybe they were Orthodox. So I went to an Orthodox church with them but it looked too weird to me… [yet] when life was difficult, I would always cry out to him [Jesus] and talk with him…" (301F)

This young Muslim woman was moved by both the conversion of her older sister and the preaching of a Russian pastor:

"In 1996 my sister became a believer. In 1999 I went to New Life church [a Russian Charismatic church] with her… I liked it so much there, Maxim [a Russian pastor] was preaching there, and I really enjoyed it. And I thought, 'I would rather come here than smoke, drink and do other things'. But I still resisted a little bit. Then my sister brought me the Bible. I was afraid to touch it, because I thought that God might punish me. But then I thought, well, everyone reads it and its Ok! So I started reading it. And I thought, 'I wish I was Russian, if I was Russian, I would accept Jesus right away!' I thought he was only for Russians and Europeans. But we are Muslims and we must believe in Muhammad. So in kept crying, why am I not Russian? I wish I could accept Jesus!" (402F)

And one final narrative excerpt on the topic of Russian agency in which it becomes clear that some Muslims, their conversion story is really the story of their interaction with Russian Christians:

"When we moved here [the capital city] in 1985 there was a Russian family living here. Their father was a Baptist pastor and his kids always said, 'There is God!' People didn't like Baptists in the Soviet Union. His daughters' classmates were my friends, and when the teacher said, 'There is no God'; this girl would stand up and say, 'There IS God!' I remember that no one liked this Baptist family. I was among them, too, but I think that they were praying for me. I mocked them but their father never came to me and said nothing. He was a pastor in a near-by city. I think they were praying for me. In 1990 I was in the army, it was still Soviet Union, and there was also a Baptist. He would open the Bible and talked about it. Then I came home from the army, I worked some and then I was put into a hospital, and there was another Baptist! He was a young man. He was supposed to go to army. So myself and another man tried to tempt him, we asked girls to go and kiss him, but he was very strong. He wouldn't give in! No matter how much we tried to make him fall. I think all these people prayed." (414M)

When everything fell apart economically in 1993, he found himself in a city far away from home. While trying to catch a train back he was robbed. Now penniless, his spiritual encounters with Russians continue:

> "So I walked into the station, and in order to hide from the police, I walked into the middle of the building. And suddenly an old Baptist woman came to me. She just sat next to me while I was thinking about my problem. I didn't ask her anything - she was Russian - and she started telling me about her life and what she was and what Jesus had done for her. Since I grew up among Russian, I knew an Orthodox guy there and he used to tell me that Orthodox cross themselves like this, and Catholics cross themselves like this. So when I heard this grandmother say 'Jesus', I looked around very carefully to make sure there were no Uzbeks or other Muslims, and I crossed myself three times, like that Russian Orthodox told me when we were children. Then I said, 'Jesus, help me!'" (414M)

Later he ended up in jail for robbery and guess who he found there? More Russian Baptists:

> "Then I came to the capital city and everything went well there, I found a job, etc. The same year, the end of the year, a friend of mine, who we smoked marihuana with…at that time I had lost my job and had lots of problems, so this friend along with other friends invited me to work with them. They were robbing shops at that time and I joined them. We stole a lot; we organized a whole group for that. In 1994 I was put to jail for the first time. When I was in my cell, I saw a book there; it was the Gospel of John. Also, together with me there was a believer in that jail. His grandmother was a Baptist - somehow I always meet Baptists!" (414M)

It was a bit surprising, even after having previously spent over a decade living in Central Asia, to realize the magnitude of the role played by local Russian Christians, they turn up in the conversion narratives far more often, and in much more significant roles, than the foreign missionaries usually do. Although in retrospect this should not be so surprising since by definition, *russified* Muslims share many aspects of the worldview of ethnic Russians. Thus the nature of religious idea transmission between the two was not so much *cross-cultural*, but something closer to *intra-cultural*, and therefore more likely. The *Russification* process had created an environment of frequent social interaction between *russified* Muslims and ethnic Russians, and religious interaction was part of this milieu. But as we have already stated, not only were ethnic Russians active in religious transmission, but so were those Muslims who had already converted.

4.4.2 Agency by Muslim Background Converts

Perhaps one of the strongest recurrent themes in the narratives was about the role that other Muslim converts themselves play in the conversion stories. There are so many instances and varied ways that only a sampling is possible:

> "We had a Kazakh camp here, we were invited. I brought a friend with me. We met a brother from Aktobe [far West Kazakhstan] there who used to be a Muslim, his name was Daniyar. He began to explain things to us through the Quran. There was also a lot of other information and it made me more confident. I went back home after the camp. Then I met a girl through a chat room, she was a Muslim, she did *namaz* for 5 years. I began to evangelize her, while she was telling me about Muhammad. It was interesting. I found quotes for her from the Quran to prove my point about *Isa*, then history, etc. I showed her disadvantages of Islam.

So she cried and asked me to give her *Kieli Kitap* [the Kazakh Bible[68]]. Then we went to Kazakh church all together - this girl, my friend and I. there was a youth meeting, and all three of us repented. After that she always shared how *Isa* answered her prayers." (418M)

In the next two excerpts we see Muslim converts moving from simply being described as agents of conversion to having recognized in roles of Christian leadership:

"Interviewer: As you think about your spiritual life, who were the key people?

Key people in my spiritual life are Alym and Sarsengul [a Muslim convert couple]. And when I was in the capital, there was sister Sabira, she was Kazakh. She was my leader and she took good care of me. She went after me, she mentored me. She said, 'Do not leave God, and follow Him!' But the greatest role in my spiritual life was played by my pastors, Alym and Sarsengul. I am very grateful that I met them.

Interviewer: Throughout this time, did any foreigners play a role in your spiritual life, or not? Any missionaries?

No, they didn't." (410F)

Not only do we see former Muslims being viewed as Christian leaders by fellow Muslim converts, as in the story above. But next we see them as officially recognized leaders of a Christian church and the joint agency of Russian Christians and former Muslims sharing lead role in a narrative. It is so insightful that it is worth looking at some length:

---

[68] *Kieli Kitap* literally means "Holy Book" but is printed on the cover of the Bible in several Turkic languages therefore has become a synonym for the English word "Bible."

"In our apartment block there was a Russian woman who was a believer but she never told us about that before because I was drunk every time she saw me…But one day she came down to our place and my wife opened the door to her with a New Testament [given to her by a relative] in her hands. That neighbor's name was Marina. She asked [my wife], 'Rimma, do you read the New Testament?' – Yes, so she began to tell my wife more about Jesus and how he saves us. Then she said, we have a small home church, do you want to come? So my wife started going there and a month later she accepted Jesus. She basically accepted Him even before, she just didn't know all of the details. So she repented there and kept going there secretly. All of a sudden she started wearing a scarf—it was a traditional Pentecostal church—Anyway, I asked her, 'Why are you wearing that scarf?' She said, 'Because I found out that I need to cover my head when I pray to God'.

'What God!?' she said, '*Yesus*'. I asked, 'You mean *Yesus*, the God of Russians!?' She said, no he is not God of Russians. I said, 'yes, he is, He is God of the Orthodox Russians!' I said, 'Stop it! This is such a disgrace! You are not going there again!' For a year, until about 1993 I was persecuting her. It was hell on earth for her." (305M)

However, his story took a dramatic turn when later feel grievously ill:

"I was sick and lying in bed for 15 days and hadn't eaten anything. I hardly drank anything, I lost maybe 20 kilos, and relatives came and said that I was going to die. So they were going to inform my parents. So my wife was crying and then went to the ministers [of her Russian church] and asked them to come and pray in our house…One was 60 years old, Tajik[69], the other one was Russian. I asked, 'What do you want?' 'Do you want God to heal you? [I thought] What an interesting question! Of course I do!' So the older man, the Tajik said, 'There is a condition!' 'What condition?' I asked. I can still remember than old man, he is

---

[69] Tajiks are a local Persian nationalities that live in Central Asia. They are historically Muslim.

with the Lord now. He said, you must forgive those who have hurt you, then we will pray for your. I said, 'Is this it?' So I closed my eyes and saw like a film of people whom I have hurt and who have hurt me. After that they laid hands on me and started praying. After about 5 minutes… this Tajik man said, 'Thank you, but we must go. We have other homes to visit. The Lord has healed you, Brother!'…

[After they left] I asked my wife, 'Who are these? Hypnotists?' She said, no they are minsters. I asked, 'Who in the world are ministers?' She said, well they are our pastors. 'Who are pastors?' 'Well, they are our leaders'. So we talked for half an hour and suddenly I felt hungry. So she brought me some water and rice water to start with, since I haven't eaten for 2 weeks… This was Saturday night. The next morning I took a nice shower, shaved, drank some tea with honey…Then I said to my wife, 'Call my driver.' So she did and then I took the phone and said to him, 'Come promptly!' He asked, 'Are you going to work?' I said, 'No, we are going to church'. He was Uzbek, so he was puzzled. 'Church? What church? You mean mosque?' 'No, it's a church!' He said, 'Maybe you shouldn't go there?' 'Don't argue with me, just come!' So our whole family went to the car and went to church. She was so happy; I can remember her happy face. So we came to church, and Ismail [the Tajik] and Gena [the Russian] were the leaders. Ismail was preaching…In the end they asked if anyone wanted to repent and reconcile with God, with Jesus. I don't know how I came forward but I did." (305M)

It may seem strange to those unacquainted with the region but here in one personal narrative we see older Muslim man led to convert to Christ at the preaching of a former Muslim who was the co-pastor of a Russian Pentecostal church! This odd kaleidoscope paints a picture of some of the ways that *Russification* has impacted the religious scene in post-Soviet Central Asia.

In the following narratives we open another aspect of agency by Muslm background converts, that is among their own family members, something that is a major theme of many interviews:

> "Interviewer: When did you first hear about Isa?
>
> Thirteen years ago.
>
> Interviewer: How did that happen?
>
> Our uncle came from Chimkent (a city in Western Kazakhstan). He accepted *Isa* there and went to church. So he came and said that we need to hear about *Isa* who died for you and you need to accept His sacrifice. So I did. Not at first, I resisted for a long time. But then I accepted Christ." (407F)

In this next extended excerpt, we see agency for conversion moving back and forth among Muslim family members:

> "I cannot tell you for sure if I was a Muslim or not, I guess I was because I was born that way... Then my brother became a believer...He came to my house many times and every time he preached... I was the last one in our family who accepted Jesus. My family did, then my wife did and then I was the last one to accept.
>
> Interviewer: So after a while when your entire family became believers, were your relatives against you?
>
> No. Nobody was ever against us; my mother even went to Bishkek (the capital of Kyrgyzstan) at that time and she would even say to her relatives, 'If you don't know *Isa*, you don't know God!' They were surprised, 'Does God have a Son?'

> We usually try to be very careful, find the right approach, but my wife was always straight forward." (409M)

It is clear that often the "agency" of Muslim converts meant spreading their new faith within existing social networks, in many cases among their extended family. This is a well known phenomena because the role of social networks in religious conversion is one of the most well established findings in the sociology of religion (Smilde (2005) cited in Kane and Park 2009, p. 367), and new converts almost always have preexisting ties to members of the new movement (Lofland and Stark 1965) (Stark 1996).

These interviews make a grounded connection between social network theory and "missionary" expansion of the gospel in new environments. It also thoroughly refutes the common misnomer which we addressed earlier, that foreign missionaries are the primary agents of conversion in "missionary" environments. Perhaps the reason many social scientists have failed to make this connection before is that the seminal work of people like James Lofland and Rodney Stark was done among new religious movements in North America.

Furthermore, Indian theologian Sathianathan Clarke takes up this issue of local agency in his study of conversions in India. He says that when emphasis in popular discourse is placed on foreign missionary agents it causes us to "fall into the Orientalist's pitfall" and "devalues the instrumentality of the native subjects themselves." He goes even further and asserts that in some of the large-scale conversion movements of the twentieth century, "the presumptive converts initially took the most active part, not the mission workers" (2003, p.336). And as a final on this important theme, Lamin Sanneh, himself a convert from Islam to Christ, argues that the reason we have tended to think of foreign missionaries as the "actors' while converts are acted upon, is because scholars have tended to focus on "the priority of foreign transmission rather than local reception" (2008, p. 131).

Chapter 5 – Findings and Analysis—Miscellaneous

This chapter will continue to explore findings and analysis as did the previous chapter, however, whereas the findings in chapter 4 where all loosely related to *Russification*, the findings in this chapter do not relate to any one specific theme.

5.1 Conversion as Spiritual Migration

One of the challenges to constructing a more field-grounded model of conversion is that the models best-known in academia are often difficult to operationalize. An example is that of Lewis Rambo's well-known sequential model of conversion which delineates the convert's movement through a series of seven stages. Rambo's model is helpful when we wish to think *abstractly* about conversion, but *in toto* it is too complex to apply to field data. Thus when a researcher in the field attempts to work with Rambo's model, they are left to try some sort of piecemeal approach, using bits and pieces of the theory as they fit the situation; therefore, the theory loses some of its explanatory power, which is based on the whole.

One way to remain closer to the field data, yet push into higher orders of thinking about the text, is through the use of metaphors. Miles and Huberman have emphasized the importance of using metaphors as "decentering devices." They can help the researcher step back from the avalanche of observations and data, and ask themselves important questions like, "what is going on here?" and "what is this telling me about the big picture?" Metaphors force us to go beyond simple description and move up to a more inferential level of thinking about the data. A metaphor is a half-step between the original text and the significance of the facts, and it gives structure to the meaning of the social processes observed (1994, pg. 252). With this in mind, I will begin my next theme of analysis with the use of an extended metaphor, that of "spiritual migration."

Finding 5: Within the metaphor of "spiritual migration," the factors that influence conversions to Christ in Central Asia can be categorized within the push/pull framework common to human migration studies.

In the realm of physical human migration, it is widely acknowledged that there are factors that "push" people to leave where they currently live and "pull" them toward a new a destination (Fouberg, Murphy, and de Blij 2012, pp 88-93). In most if not all cases, human migration is caused by some combination of both factors - some from the "push" category and some from the "pull." In the same way, the conversion stories in this study demonstrated some factors that "pulled" them toward faith in Christ, or the community of his followers, and other factors that should be understood as "pushing" them away from the Central Asian *islam* they knew.

5.1.1 Push Factors

Before going any further, it is important to clarify the "location" from which these factors are "pushing." As I have repeatedly stated in this thesis, we are specifically looking at conversion in the context of Central Asian *islam,* i.e. the local manifestation of Islam which we have carefully detailed in earlier sections of this work. That means we are actually talking about people reacting against the complex of cultural behaviors and values with which they were raised more than we are talking about Islam proper, or even *islam* local.

In introducing this idea, I will group these "push" factors together. However, one interview contained such a succulent illustration of a "push" that I felt compelled to use it despite the fact that it really does not fit into any of my other categories:

> "One time I was standing waiting for my granddaughters. They were supposed to come back from school. They had to pass by a mosque behind a bridge. At five o'clock, people were leaving the mosque. There is a big channel there, giving pure water to several villages. These people threw chewing tobacco into that water before going in, and then coming back, they were spitting into the river. I was very angry but couldn't say anything because there were several of them. So I just stood there while waiting for my grandchildren. But that kind of attitude made me wonder, 'Why do believers like them do that?' They do it because they say 'If you bring offerings, it removes God's anger from you'. So, if you bring offerings, you can do anything; it's sort of like bribing God. So, in the Islamic world people do not change but they feel free to do whatever because all they need to do is bring offering and they will be released from their sin. So they remain sinful and never change. That's their main principle. They feel free to spit into water that others drink. All of them did! That really disgusts me, and pushes me away from Islam." [emphasis mine] (208M)

This participant clearly articulated what others left implicit, that certain behaviors in their "Muslim" society caused them to lose interest in the ways of life handed down from their forefathers. This obvious disregard for the health and wellbeing of others, rooted in a theological framework, was one of several factors that have the ability to "push" even a 70-year-old Muslim man away from the religion of his ancestors. Now let us examine other ingredients in the mix, which have done the same to other Muslims in the region.

Religious Nominalism

The most common "push" factor was religious nominalism. As we have demonstrated repeatedly in this thesis, by the end of Soviet rule, Islam in Central Asia was only a shadow of the worldwide faith rooted in the fiery words of "the Apostle of Allah," and had become something of an ethnic marker for most people. Nevertheless, in order to give a completely accurate picture, we should first look at examples of the few cases where study participants came from more observant backgrounds:

> "We were growing up thinking of ourselves as Muslims. Not just our ancestors, but my father was practicing *namaz* prayer. He made my mother read *namaz* and wear *hijab*. He was searching for God. My mother read *namaz* and they both told me that when I will turn 12, I will also read namaz and wear hijab." (204F)

And:

> "When I was growing up he [my father] did namaz but he wasn't so strict about observing all the rules. But now he is much more fundamental. He observes all customs, traditions and rituals; he prays five times a day. He is very strong about it… My father went to Mecca for pilgrimage. He prays five *namaz* prayers. He observes all Muslim rituals." (203M)

Two things are important to note. First, these interviews represent a wife and husband. Second notice *when* this man's father became really observant, it was later, presumably after the fall of the Soviet Union, thus after the study participant's formative years. But even then these are non-typical cases from the study. Religious nominalism was such a common part of the narratives that it only takes a few examples to give the sense of this issue:

> "Of course, we always followed Islamic traditions, like we did circumcision. We had one mullah in the village that would come and do all the rituals. We of course thought of ourselves as Muslims and separated ourselves from the Russians who we saw as Christians. We did follow all the rituals but we didn't have a real spiritual life. I personally never went to mosque… Overall, we called ourselves Muslims only because of our ethnicity." (103M)

> "During the Soviet times, as I remember, my parents were no Muslims… they were just typical Soviet, secular people. They didn't have any spiritual books at home… And so I just hadn't heard about God at all." (201M)

And:

> "My father died two years ago. I think it was God's will. He was full of sin. He was an alcoholic. He himself never went to the mosque, never prayed, but he was so against my belief in *Isa*." (407F)

This last excerpt raises an issue that may sound strange in a Muslim society, alcoholism; although it may sound unusual, that is the next "push" factor we will examine.

Alcoholism

Muslim scholar Adeeb Khalid, author of *Islam after Communism* tells an insightful story in the introduction to his book. He recounts his first encounter with fellow Muslim scholars in Central Asia, at a university cafeteria. His new friends were "particularly delighted that their interlocutor was Muslim." So after he sat down to eat, "a few minutes later, my new acquaintances joined me unbidden at my table, armed with a bottle of Vodka. Their delight at meeting me was sincere, and they were completely unself-conscious about the oddity of lubricating the celebration of our acquaintance with copious amounts of alcohol" (2007, p.1). By the end of that era, alcoholism had left a deep scar on the peoples of the Soviet Union; it had even become entrenched among the Muslims of Central Asia. It was referred to in many of the interviews, where participants discussed either their own struggles with it, or its detriment to their natal family through the drinking of their "Muslim" parents. It often was one of the things that "pushed" people to look for a better way of life:

> "My father came from China. He came over the border in the 1960s... In China my grandfather, my father's father, studied in a special Islamic school in those times. My Dad, for the first few years followed all of the rituals and prayed five times, but then he quit and lived his own life. He died early, when he was 50. My mother was young, only 40, with seven kids. When my father died, my mother was alone with seven children. It was very hard because our mother began to drink after our Dad died, and she drank for many years." (412F)

The next except reveals the deep emotional harm that children of alcoholics experience, and helps us understand why this should be thought of as a factor that often "pushed" people away from their parents' way of life to search for answers in a new faith:

> "I grew up in the actually simple family. My mom was working in the shop, my dad was working. It was a simple family. My mom did all responsibility for the family because my father was alcoholic actually. He was a drunk and we did not have peace in our home. I don't remember when we were all together like a family, father mother, myself sitting together at the table eating. I don't really

remember this kind of time. I remember when I went first to the school; it was first grade, the first of September. My mom brought me to the school and said 'wait for your father when all your lessons will be finished. Wait for father and he will pick you up.' So I was the last on in the class. Nobody came to take me from the school. I went home by myself. I was so angry. I remember this feeling still. I was so angry, like nobody could come to take me. So when I was walking, when I was closer to my house I heard my father's voice, and I understood that he was at home and I was completely destroyed at that time. I remember I knocked and he opened the door. He was drunk, and it was so painful to me. Since that time I had like not good experience toward my father." (405F)

And one more common factor that pushed people away from Islam.

Unanswered Existential Questions

"I remember when I got married, it was a bad marriage. He was my neighbor… I remember when I accepted Jesus as my Savior; it was an interesting day. I said to God that day, 'Why is my life so difficult? Why do I have to suffer all the time? Why did you even create us, people?' Because my first husband was a drug addict and it was very hard. Because when my father died, I was 11; and then when I was 16-17, my sister died; she was 25 at that time. Then I married this drug addict. So when I came to God I kept asking him, why do I suffer so much in this life? Why am I here? So I was walking down the street and talking to God like this." (412F)

"Interviewer: How long did it take between the time when you first heard, and when you actually accepted Jesus?

This was also the time of searching. I was thinking about God. I was wondering why there were so many religions and why God allowed such an atmosphere. So I began to seek truth. That was the period of search. That's when I became disappointed in Islam because I could not find answers to many questions I was wondering about. So I started learning more about Christianity, even though I did not make a choice yet. But a friend who became a Christian, her name was Ira, said, 'Just pray to God and He will direct you and show you the truth.' After I prayed like that, God began to guide me towards Christianity." (101F)

"Interviewer: Did you go to mosque to hear the Quran?

No, I didn't but I met with people from there. I tried to follow things that they told me but when I would fail to pray, for example, the fourth or the fifth time, I would feel heavy in my heart. I would get depressed because I could not please God. So gradually I became disappointed because I felt like Allah was far away, that he didn't care about me, so he intentionally created all these hard laws that were impossible to observe. So I was thinking that I was going to hell, not to heaven because I could not follow these laws, which meant I was guilty. Over time I became disappointed in Islam but I kept searching… I was 18. So I started at 15 when I started asking questions like "why do people die, where do we go after death etc.?" These fears always made me ask these questions. So I thought about poverty, good and evil, injustice, etc. These questions make us think about God." (206M)

Gooren theorized that people become religious seekers when they become dissatisfied with the meanings generated by their natal religion (2007, p. 339). And so, stripped of the spiritual resources which it had built-up over the previous millennia, it should not be surprising that such nominal Muslims were left with deep unanswered questions about life's transcendent dimensions, or that they were highly susceptible to widespread social ills like alcoholism. Nor should it surprise us that these interrelated issues caused a deep dissatisfaction with the life and pushed people toward something else.

However, the factors that motivate people to migrate are complex and intertwined. When people make major changes such as physical—or spiritual—moves, they are not always sure of what the individual factors are that motivated them (Datta 2004). That is why human geographers always speak of "push-pull" factors in one breath. Therefore, we must be careful that we do not over-dissect these push factors, and quickly move to those that the interviews revealed as "pulling" people toward faith in Christ.

5.1.2 Pull Factors

What did converts find attractive enough to risk the disapproval, even persecution, of family and community, by turning to Christ? The interviews point to several factors, which we will explore below. One that appeared commonly in the data has to do with the attraction of people with a good reputation:

Good Reputation of Christians

In chapter 4 we examined the "agency" of Russian Christians, often Baptists; it is a fact that many of the narratives portrayed them as the main proponents of religious change. Therefore it is not surprising to find that one of the pull factors was the good reputation Russian Baptists:

> "After [my] conversion I said, 'I felt I needed to share with someone,' so I went to my mother and asked her to sit down, and didn't know how to tell her that I believed in Jesus. I didn't know how to share the Gospel so I simply said, 'Mother, I have become Baptist'. She sat and thought about it and then she said, 'Well, Baptists don't steal, don't drink and don't lie'. It turned out that at her work she had some Baptist colleagues, and as she observed them, they were a real testimony to her. They would always be honest with money, and kept their promises. So even though I didn't know the rules of Christian living, I started doing what my mother said she saw those Baptists do. Even though my mother was not a believer but she saw how they lived." (303M)

> "Our father always thought well of Baptist believers. He liked that fact that they always told the truth. Not Orthodox Christians but Baptists. He always said that he respected them." (406M)

However, it was not just the good reputation of Russian Baptists that proved a powerful draw, but even more often it was an attraction to the lives of those Muslims who had already converted to Christ:

> "It was in 1994. That's when I first heard about Jesus and came to Him. I came with a friend. It was a Pentecostal church in Bishkek. I really liked it, I felt welcomed there. Local Kyrgyz believers were very warm and called me 'brother'. I thought, 'wow, they are very welcoming!'" (419M)

Or when it is a member of their own family who demonstrates obvious changes:

> "Before I came to God my husband drank a lot. He was an alcoholic…I was so irritated with him and I was so angry that every time he came home drunk I would scold and curse him both in Russian and in Uyghur. So my older daughter always told me, 'Mom, how can you say such words, you were a primary school teacher

for eight years!' I said, 'I just cannot stand it when he comes drunk!' The day I came to Jesus, He also healed my tongue. I stopped using that dirty language. My oldest daughter saw that change and she said after two weeks, 'Mom, can I come to that group with you?' At that time I was going every week. I said, 'Why?' She said, 'Well, it must be a very good place. You have stopped cursing!' So she went with me and also repented. After two months I think, my younger daughter also repented, and we started a home group at our house." (404F)

Or this man, who converted in his 60s, and only after more than ten years of opposing his wife, who converted first:

"The greatest testimony to me was my wife. She was changing right in front of me. She became very obedient. She became gentle, very different. I thought, 'Maybe she is pretending so that I would come to this Russian God?' But God began to change me." (305M)

As we explored in chapter 4, the hybrid nature of a *russified* identity made all things Russian more acceptable. This likely made it relatively easy for highly *russified* Muslims to be drawn by the good reputation of Russian Baptists, a reputation which appears to have been widely held in society. Nevertheless, the "pull" of a good reputation becomes even closer to home when it is manifested by a convert, someone in their own social networks. Lofland and Stark called this the draw of positive deviant behavior (1965). That is, although an ethnic Kyrgyz or Uzbek professing faith in Christ is a social deviant, the influence of their good behavior is even more significant because they are supposed to be social deviants; thus, their behavior should be bad or wrong. One study participant seemed to intuitively understand this:

> "I always say that we need to be careful because [the] Islamic spirit is very strong here. People think God is very far away and they can come to Him through rituals, Namaz, etc. So I give them information about the living God little by little. They observe how I live, they see my children, they say, 'Your children never say bad words; they never fight, they are very obedient'. So they see the character of Jesus in my family. It makes me very happy; it's like a letter to them." (408F)

Now we turn to the final pull factor that we will examine.

The Supernatural

The experience of an event perceived of as having a supernatural origin was a very common aspect of the conversion narratives I studied. Not only that, but these occurrences formed the core of several stories. Under this rubric of "supernatural" I have included dreams, visions, physical healings, as well as other things that are hard to classify. Due to the nature of the healing stories, the excerpts are rather long:

> "One time one of our brothers got sick, he fell in the kindergarten and he injured his head. After that he had trouble sleeping at night, cried a lot from headaches. We took him to doctors, did tests and check-ups but doctors could not determine what was wrong with him. But something was wrong. We took him to a therapist and psychologist but had no results, nobody knew what was wrong and what his diagnosis was… Since in the medical field nothing could be done; she tried the Muslim way but it didn't make him better but rather, it made things worst and worst. He was very young then; he would hit people, he could not recognize himself or us; it was hard. And what's interesting, it only happened at nights. During the day he was a normal child. My mother was very tired. She tried

everything - medical things, Muslim things; what else could she do? What were her other options? At that time there was an American family in our neighborhood. They didn't tell us at that time but they were missionaries. They just moved to our neighborhood to live. They said they wanted to learn more about the culture, the people and the national system of these neighborhoods. So, my mother and we all became friends with them. One day my mother could not take it anymore and she shared her problem with them. She said, this is what's been happening with my son and I don't know what to do. They said to us, 'We will be praying for you...' Several days later the wife came to us and this time she was sharing with us more openly. She said, 'Let me pray for this child for God to make him OK. It was in the evening. They prayed for our family and for my little brother and that night my brother slept all night through. He slept well and quietly till very morning. We were shocked; my Mom was shocked; she said, 'How is this possible? We tried everything - we took him to doctors, we read the Koran over him but all in vain. My mother ran to their house and asked, 'What did you do? What did you do to my son? He slept all night long! That's when they started telling us about *Isa*. (202F)

This next woman read some Christian literature right before she was scheduled to have surgery. While sitting in the hospital she started thinking about what she had read:

"The evening before that I read the brochure and there was the sinner's prayer in the end; I even learned it by heart. So I was sitting and thinking, 'God, if you are so good and loving—our family always believed in God, my father always said that there is God—so I thought, Why do I have to have this surgery? It says here that you are able to heal; why don't you heal me?' So while we were sitting and waiting for this nurse, who was supposed to take me up for the surgery, I actually began to talk with God out loud... My daughter asked, 'Mother, who are you talking to?' I said, 'I am talking with God. It says in this booklet that He is loving and he heals, so I am wondering, why do I have to have this surgery? I love God and I always knew He exists.' Then the nurse came and said that the professor who was supposed to do the surgery left for the capital city. This doctor was the best and we agreed to pay him a lot of money to do the surgery. She said, 'He will be back in a week. Do you think you can wait? Or else, you can stay here, we have other good doctors.' But I said, 'No! I will wait for this professor'. She said, 'You will have to go without food because you are having an aggravation of your kidney stone disease right now.' I said, 'It's okay; I will just drink water, but I want to wait for this doctor.' This was March 1st and they told me to come on March 9th. So I went back home." (404F)

Then her sister told her about a church she had been attending:

"She started telling me about their pastor, about their home group, she said that she's been going there, and there are primarily Muslims there—Kazakhs and Uyghurs, Tatars, and some Russians. She said that people there receive healing and she told me about a woman who received healing of tongue cancer there. She said, 'If you would like, we could go and meet with the pastor. He will explain you everything, because I cannot explain…' He was Kazakh…So we went there, and from 6 to 10 pm he talked with us. He explained who is Jesus, etc. So I believed then… Anyway, after the sermon they invited people who want to receive healing to come forward. I was the first one to come. My sister grabbed me and said, 'Don't go!' But I did anyway. They started praying. Then He said directly to me, in Russian, 'Do you know that Jesus is Lord?' I said, 'No, I don't.' I wanted to say, Muhammad, because I believed I was a Muslim. He said, 'I explained to you yesterday and I explained to you today, Jesus is Lord! Did you come for healing? Do you believe that God only heals through Jesus Christ? Unless we say his name, God will not heal you.' I said, 'Okay'…So he laid his hand on me and simply prayed. He said, 'I command to these stones to become sand and come out. Thank you that you have healed her!' And he went to pray for someone else, for a girl… But I felt fire coming from my head to my toes and leave me. As he was praying, I felt like a little fish inside me. That was the sensation I had. So I received healing after that prayer. I never had a surgery… So God healed me supernaturally. After one month I decided to do another ultrasound and I went to the same place where I did it before, to confirm. So the doctor asked, 'Did you have a surgery?' I said, No. The doctor said, 'You don't have any stones!' So I told him, 'I went to believing people, they prayed for me and I received healing. I came to you to confirm that'. So he gave me an official medical certificate that said that I really was healed." (404F)

Next are dreams, and again they require an extended narrative to allow us to grasp the full impact they must have had on the convert:

"We were like most Muslims here. I never counted *namaz* or went to the mosque. I became a thief…Not long after I got to prison (the second time) I had a dream. It was just like it was real life; it still feels real to me. I was standing there watching this huge chasm and people were being thrown into it. They were screaming and it was horrible. I knew that they were being thrown into hell. Then I watched this one man being thrown in, but suddenly *Isa* caught him as he was falling and pulled him to himself, then tossed him up into the sky and the man went to heaven.

I knew this man was *Isa*, I don't know how, but I did. He was wearing a white robe and a turban. I just stood there and watched him grab people who were falling into hell, and he was saving them. Each one, pulling them to himself and then tossing them into heaven. I remember marveling, "How powerful he is to save them! What a wonderful savior *Isa* is! He is so strong he saves them from hell…'

Interviewer: How did you know about Isa?

I knew that he was one of our prophets, and I knew that he was like the Russian God. That is what all of us call *Yesus*, the Russian God. But I knew that he was really one of our prophets.

Then five years go by of my seven and one-half year sentence, and I have another dream. This one was so frightening. It was so real. I saw myself escaping from the prison. I slipped out of the fence and was walking across the space between the two fences. In our prisons it is like this [making a diagram out of table items], there is one fence, then a space, then another fence. The guards sit in the towers on the first inside fence.

I was walking across the space between the fences and then I heard the guard shout at me, 'Stop! Stop or I will shoot you!' I heard him cock his automatic, and felt the fear, but I kept running. Then I heard the sound of his shots from the automatic and I could even feel the pain of bullets hitting me on this side in the back [touching his right lower back].

Then suddenly everything was black. I could not move because I could feel things very close to me. Then slowly there was light, a small candle in a chai bowl, and I could see that I was in the grave. I was laying there in my naked flesh, in the grave with a small candle by me. I could not move my arms or body but I knew I was buried. I started to cry out, but no one could hear me. I cried out 'Oh Allah, forgive me! Please Allah, forgive me!' This I shouted over and over. I was terrified because I was in the grave, but no one was listening to my screams. Then I awoke in my cell. I was terrified. It was awful. I was thinking, what does this mean? You know we believe that dreams are important, and I was very fearful about what this one meant. Was I about to die? Was something bad going to happen to me? I just did not know. Then I remembered the dream about *Isa* from five years before. I wondered how he saved people from hell." (205M)

In these cases, the dreams came before conversion, pulling them toward a change of religions. In the examples below, the dreams came after the converts had made an initial decision, during difficulty, and strengthened their resolve. The following example comes from a time of confusion in the convert's life, when the local community was threatening to kill him:

> "I officially repented in the church; it was in December, 1994. Later on, when persecution started, I went back home and hid for six months and didn't want to see anyone. I was scared. Muslim Uyghurs wanted to kill me. They threatened all Uyghur believers. They said, 'We will kill you and your entire family; you have betrayed Islam!'
>
> Robert [an American missionary] came looking for me, but because he didn't know that I was living separately, he only came to my parents' house. Even when I was at my parents' house and knew that Robert was there, I stayed in my room because I didn't want problems.
>
> Then I had a dream. Jesus came to me; my spirit was awake. I could sense that someone came into my room. I heard a lot of noise, like someone was breaking things. It sounded like an earthquake. I was scared. I heard a voice, 'Go to Robert!' The voice sounded like rushing water, like the Bible says. He didn't even tell His name. But I knew who he was. I woke up; it was very quiet. It was 3 am; I had peace in my heart. I told my daughter, 'Jesus came to me at night; I could feel it in my spirit. His voice was like waterfall.' After that my life changed; fear was gone." (420M)

And finally, here is an account that combines a dream and a physical healing soon after this woman had converted:

> "I also got a videotape in Uyghur with Jesus film, I was very interested. In the end, when Jesus was crucified, and He was in the cross, I was very upset. 'Why

did they do that to Him? He didn't do anything wrong. Why isn't He coming down from the cross?' Later my friend came and told me about Jesus; that He died for our sins, and I accepted Him. Later on, my mother's younger brother died of a disease. My mother was grieving terribly and she had a heart attack. She laid there and didn't move; we gave her water in a spoon. We sat with her till morning. Then I read this book in Uyghur, the gospel of John. And my sister did too, and she said, 'This would be so wonderful if Jesus could just come and lay hands on our Mom, and she would be healed'. I kept reading and after everyone went to bed I started praying hard at her bed. At that time I didn't know how to pray because I was a new believer. So I prayed hard, 'Jesus, heal my Mom!' My eyes were closed and I saw a vision. I saw a lot of dry, scary-looking trees. It was dark and a wind was blowing. I came out to a road and saw a car coming. There was a strong light shining into my eyes. I opened my eyes and realized that our house was filled with that light, just for a second, and it was gone. That light was very bright. It illuminated the entire house. I sensed peace in my heart; I was confident that God will heal my mother… Two days later my Mom began to recover; she started talking. Then she got up and started walking. She recovered quite quickly. Later on, my younger sister was diagnosed with cancer. She had a tumor here, and doctors said it was cancer. So we went to Almaty with her, and there they said, 'Yes, there is tumor but we will have to do some further tests to see if it is cancer or not'. My sister was standing there, crying, and I started praying. 'God, please make this cancer go away from my sister, my family and our generation'. When we did an X-ray in our village, there was tumor. But now that we were in Almaty and they said that she needed to make a scan, and when we did, there was no tumor. So God did a miracle." (410F)

Obviously, the physical healings recounted in these stories could have psychosomatic explanations, and the dreams could be no more than evidence of extreme psychological duress. In fact, all the accounts of supernatural "pull" factors could be explained away if that is what one cares to do. Therefore it is essential, before going any further, that we determine a framework through which to think about such unverifiable reports of the supernatural. As a *social*, not physical, scientist, I contend that rather than thinking in terms of verifiable facts[70], the most profitable thing to do is to consider how the events were interpreted in relation to conversion.

William Clark has written about the significance of dreams and visions as a rationale for conversion among Muslims of the former Soviet Union. Specifically, he contends they have a long established tradition of receiving supernatural communication from God; therefore, dreams are often woven into conversion stories as part of the basis for conversion (2009 pp. 135-6). However, we must not think of this as something unique to the spread of Christianity in Central Asia. In writing about the early centuries of the Christian era, Lamin Sanneh says, "Visions, dreams, ecstasy, exorcism, and healings featured prominently in the mission of Christianity for many centuries (2008, p. 59). If this type of experience seems strange to those more familiar with the modern Western Church, then perhaps it is a sign that Christian expression in Central Asia is returning to its original Eastern roots.

Of course, "spiritual migration" with its push-pull factors is only one possible metaphor for understanding the conversion narratives in this study. In the next section we will explore then from a slightly different angle.

---

[70] Verification of the supernatural is by definition an oxymoron. For example, while we could, in this case, verify that the woman's mother had a heart attack, and we might be able to verify that she recovered. However, there is no way to prove or disprove the *means* of that recovery. Whether was completely a natural process, the result of medical treatment, or even a sign of divine intervention, these are completely beyond the realm of scientific certitude.

5.2 The Three Languages of Conversion

As I stated in chapter three on methodology, one of the sub-categories of Narrative Inquiry I have used is Holistic-Content (HC) analysis. This approach has the goal of finding a holistic impression of individual narratives which harmonizes the narrative whole with its various parts and focuses on larger, thematic elements. While not all of the narratives in the study have the strong, cohesive themes required for this approach, several do, and using Holistic-Content analysis was quite profitable on these. It enables the researcher to step back far enough from the details to conceptualize higher levels of abstraction. One particular abstraction in this data set that I believe to be quite important is what I have called the "languages of conversion." This expression helps capture the idea that the way people use language is a key insight into their systems of meaning (Lieblich, Tuval-Machiach & Zilber 1998), a foundational principal of Narrative Inquiry.

Finding 6: Conversion narratives often have major, overarching themes—or "languages" through which they are told. For Central Asian Muslims converting to Christ, three of these were most common; the language of joining, the language of rejecting, and the language of believing.

It should be pointed out that these three "languages" are not mutually exclusive. Converts often make statements that fit into two, or even all three categories, over the course of the interview. However, several of the interviews were typified by a certain "language," it being the primary way that people verbally reconstructed their conversions.

5.2.1 Language of Joining

The Western world has been deeply shaped by individualism, to such an extent that we often view religious conversion exclusively through the lens of the individual. In contrast to that, many of those in this study framed their conversion in a communal sense. This does not mean they were part of a "group conversion" of some sort, rather, that they explained their experience of conversion in such a way as to highlight the desire to belong to a new community rather than other potential dimensions of the decision. It is important to remember that individualized religiosity has no precedent in most societies (Hefner 1993, p. 116), something particularly true of traditional, closely-knit communities such as Muslims in Central Asia. Thus for some, conversion *had to be* the joining of a new community. The following series of excerpts from a single interview show the way this attraction to a group unfolded over time in one convert's life:

> "The Soviet Union collapsed and we got independence a few months later. This was in 1991. And as soon as, ah the Soviet Union collapsed, I remember they started to be, my parents started to be interested in Islam… [my father told me] 'Now we've got independence and the government is encouraging people to find their beliefs, to believe what the ancestors believed.' And they started sharing from the book [Quran]… And being at the age 15-16, I was the kind of person, just like any average boy, I was interested in things other than this. This was something boring to me…" (201M)

So as teenagers often do, he started distancing himself from his family, but particularly from his natal religion. Then a few years later as a university student:

> "In 1993, when I was a freshman in the university when a lady [a foreigner] came, and so a lesson was canceled and [they set-up] a lecture hall for about 100 people,

you can imagine. And a lady came and spoke about Jesus and Mohammad. And she spoke about who was Jesus and who was Muhammad. And she came with a stack of books and she said, "You students are welcome to come to my desk and pick up these books; they are free." And when the students heard "free" many of them were curious, although many of them just took books [and] just tore them and threw them away… These events made become acquainted with Jesus. I became aware of Jesus… But I didn't consider myself Christian… I wanted to find answers... But I still considered myself Muslim." (201M)

Here he becomes "acquainted with Jesus" in the context where many other university students, though not all, were also showing interest. However, his level of interest in Christianity remained minimal until he moved to the capital city:

"So, this was also the year when my wife and I were separated. And I moved to the capital city from my small hometown to start a career, to start a new, to make a new family. And being in the capital, I wanted to find two things. I wanted to find a job, and I wanted to find a wife. As I mentioned, I found a job in Christian organization. This was the first time I got a Bible… Then I was invited to this 'youth church.'

Interviewer: A very western style church?

Very western style. And I really liked it. And since I joined an American organization I wanted to improve my English. I wanted to listen to western music; I wanted to be just like these people. Probably this was also [because] I was a provincial boy—I wanted to be like these others. Because the young people at church had many things like westerners—*JanSport* backpacks[71] and speaking English to the expat people, I was like, I also wanted to do this, to talk to people like this." (201M)

---

[71] *JanSport* was at that time a very popular American brand, similar to *Nike* or *Adidas*.

Next he displays remarkable self-awareness:

> "So maybe if I analyze myself at that time, maybe I didn't want to be different. Maybe I felt underestimated because many people from villages think of people [from the capital] like giants because that is another life. People there are smarter, people are better, [but] I came from a small town…so for this reason I did not want to miss those meetings. But at the same time was making new friends. At that time in my life I didn't have many friends. I was introverted person, very reserved. And here I met people who were very interested in my life. They would invite me places. I felt esteemed, valued. And I wanted more…
>
> Interviewer: Was getting baptized a way to identify with them, or with Jesus?
>
> Probably to identify with the church rather than Jesus. Having this western influence we almost every Sunday after the fellowship had, we walked to café and we drank Coke, had hot dogs, they were popular at that time. And I remember I wanted a *JanSport* back pack!" (201M)

Notice how a single, mass produced consumer item with a brand name, became the emotional proxy for his longing to belong to a new group, a new, globally successful spiritual "brand." Robert Hefner observed that when societies are thrust "into a larger or reorganized macrocosm," such as when Soviet Central Asia opened to the wider world, "new lifestyles and ethnical options appear. Missionaries or other proselytizers may lead in this challenge to tradition… In such a context, a religion that promises a measure of dignity and access to the values and rewards of the larger society may find a ready following" (1993, pp. 26-27).

The next example of this "language of joining" also comes from someone who encountered Christianity while a university student:

<u>"Interviewer: How did you convert? Through whom?</u>

My sister heard in the university from a local woman who came and talked about God... My sister was going to that university and went to the meeting. She said it was interesting... Later she came to another meeting for those who wanted to know more, and one day my sister invited me to a home group. At that time I didn't know that she already repented... One day she said, 'You know, there might be many of your friends there [at the meeting]; I saw a lot of young people there. Just come once and I will never ask you again'. So I thought, OK, maybe I will go just once. So when I came, there was a lot of love there, people were very kind and nice, gave me a lot of attention. That woman was there, too, playing the guitar. I especially liked one song and I asked her to sing it again. So they played that song for me several times. I liked it so much that I kept coming to that group. So after a month maybe I decided to accept the Lord. It was quick. I heard the Word there, too, but every time I came I asked them to sing 'my song' for me..." (207M)

Notice the various expressions of "joining" in this narrative. First, her sister was the one who invited her (a common element). Second, there were other university students she knew coming to the group. And finally, notice that while she mentions a more theological element, teaching from the Word (Bible), it is only in passing. She quickly reoriented her narrative toward becoming part of the group by each time she asked them to sing "my song," thus cementing her membership with them. Also, notice that there is no mention in this context of Jesus.

Later, their mother first found out that the two siblings had converted, and she threated to kill herself if they did not stop going to the church:

> "I never stopped coming because I knew it was very important. Our pastors and leaders helped us to understand how important these meetings were. They explained it well and we knew we needed to meet and hear about God and worship Him and sing and it brought us closer together." (207M)

Again the emphasis on joining is on display. When faced with a serious backlash at home, the expressed answer was not stronger faith, but closer bonds with the new group.

Our final look at the "language of joining" comes from the oldest participant in the study, a Muslim man who converted in his 70s. Interestingly, his interview is an example of two different "languages" showing up as strong themes in one narrative. First we will look at the way he framed his conversion through the language of joining:

> "Interviewer: You said that before you came to Jesus, you were watching the lives of believers very carefully. Could you explain?
>
> They were honest and open in their relationships. When I saw friends, like when your friend comes to visit you with his wife, or two friends with their wives, they were so friendly and respectful. The [newly converted] Christians would treat all women respectfully, young and old, their sisters, etc. I saw them treat women in church as they would treat their friends' wives. In a secular company when people meet like that, there is a lot of unhealthy relationships between men and women. Among Christians they were kind and respectful, never cursed, no bad words…
>
> They were sacrificial. When they would come visit us, we had no money at that time. We had a lake there and they wanted to go there but had no money. I said,

'Sorry but we have no money to give you!' They would say, 'We have no money but God is with us!' I thought, 'How is God going to give you money?' So they went and came back and when I asked how was it, they said, 'It was good, we kept meeting nice people who would help us and gave us rides…Later on when I became a believer and began to send more time with them, in a group or in a church, they became closer friends than other friends I had, very quickly. We have a brother, and we play chess 2-3 times a week. So they are better friends than my other friends who are not Christian…

"In towns in the valley there are old men who are believers there. Every other month these elders come together. It's like a meeting for 50-year olds and up. Some of them older, some are younger. But we talk together and fellowship. It's a joy to see that there are more believers of older age in these small cities, more than here in the capital. Of course here we also have some elderly believers but we don't meet here. We go there, we make pilaf, we slain a sheep and meet all together for a whole day… Anyway, these old people tell wonderful stories, it is wonderful to see that it is not just young people but also old people who become believers. And they are very strong… It would be great for you to ask these questions to these elders. Some are very old." (208M)

Clearly this gentleman was drawn to the new Christian community, particularly to people of his own age cohort. This was a common element in all three of the narratives above, participants being drawn to join those of their same age group. Lofland and Stark have theorized that sometimes religious conversion is a matter of accepting the opinions of one's friends (1965), and in socially stratified cultures like that of Muslims in Central Asia, one's friends *are* one's age cohorts; friendship outside of one's age group is almost unthinkable. Yet at the same time, this elderly convert also told his own story in the strongest terms of rejecting his natal faith.

5.2.2 Language of Rejecting

As we have emphasized throughout this thesis, conversion is not only "a turning to" something, but also "a turning from" something else (Austin-Broos 2003, p.1). In the analysis directly above, we saw some study participants focused on the group to whom they had collectively turned. In the same way, others placed the emphasis of their narrative on what they had turned from, or more accurately, what they were rejecting. These we have identified as "the language of rejection." We immediately pick up this theme by returning to the same, wide-ranging interview, that of a Muslim man who converted in his 70s, his framing of rejection centering on Islam's prophet:

> "I don't understand how Islamists explain the fact that Muhammad, being the great prophet, violated the laws of Sharia? Like, a man can have four wives but he had 11, plus two concubines. Moreover, he took a 9-year old or even a 6-year-old. So how do they explain that he could do things like that?
>
> [And] another question, related to that one. In the East it is believed that having a son is the blessing of God. He had three sons. But all three of them had died; one at 17, the other one at 18 months old, etc. So how would they explain that? If he was a man who was so close to God, it seems that God did not bless him? I've never heard this question before. I mean, I heard the story but Islamists never talked about it…
>
> My friends often ask me: you have become a Christian, they say, why do you now like our faith, since in our country it is believed that Islam is the Uzbek faith. I usually say, 'If Muhammad lived here at our time, he would have been put to prison for marrying a 9-year-old girl! In any nation, actually. That's why I do not believe in a man like that." (208M)

This rejection of his natal religious heritage could hardly be shaped into a more dramatic picture than a direct attack on the person of Muhammad! While this was certainly the most overt expression of the language of rejection, it was hardly the only one:

> "My parents were half Russian and half Uyghur, so this was also a part of the influence on my life. Because if I would grow up in a really Muslim strong family [with] Muslim relationships among relatives. But because of this, of my parents divorcing and I been grow up in an atmosphere where I wanted to find out who I am…
>
> Interviewer: When was the first time you heard about Jesus?
>
> I heard about Jesus when I became 19 yrs. old, a friend of my father who worked with him, he shared with me about the New Testament.
>
> Interviewer: A local man?
>
> Yeah, he was a Russian guy and my father was the head of the shoe company. Most of the workers my father hired were Christians… I found out after that there was some of the staff at his company in the past, they were his relatives, Muslim people, but they were always trying to not be honest with him. While he was away they cheated him… or they stole some things. It was kind of really big disappointment for my father.
>
> It was a point of big arguing for my father because he wanted to just be nice to them, but if he did, his business would not be run well. There was big pressure from elders in the family saying 'Hey, why didn't you hire my son?' and my father felt that OK, I will take it but then these guys were in his team, so he was always solving the problems, like they were bankrupt or he got them released from prison one guy, his youngest brother then the son of my step mother. So it was really hard." (306M)

Reflecting back on his youth he identifies with his father's problems and frustrations because of Muslim staff in his factory. Then after talking again about the positives of the Christian staff:

> "Inteviewer: So you were comparing these two groups?
>
> I was seeing, wow these people are praying Namaz and he is talking about another religion, talking about Jesus. This really influenced me because I can see every day and hear what is going on in these families… I did not have even a clear understanding of what is Islam. Just going to the Mosque with father and uncles, during all these Muslim festivals. Of course we were meant to be among relatives to see how they demonstrated their belief in Islam. But in life I did not see this change, it was like a hobby to them, you know. They just went to the mosque but in reality in their lifestyles I did not see any change." (306M)

His choice of words in this last excerpt are particularly insightful: "Just going to the Mosque with father and uncles, during all these Muslim festivals… to see how they demonstrated their belief in Islam." Yet it was precisely because of this "demonstration" that he became disillusioned with Islam.

However, while this rejection of natal culture and community was a major part of several narratives, it is interesting to note that in some, participants also articulated remorse for beginning their new faith in the paradigm of rejecting. The participant cited above had obviously reflected extensively on this topic:

> "Because it was a Russian speaking church [where he first attended], there was not a person who had experience working with Muslim people… [it felt like] this is the religion for Russian speaking people. But if there had been the right

explanation, that just because I [had] became a believer but I didn't have to cut off relationship with relatives." (306M)

This participant, who is now a leader among the former Muslim converts in his country, went even further to recommend a change of conversion paradigm for new converts which was much less oriented toward rejection:

"So now I am not taking new people to the church [building] because I know what it is like for them. This will bring a not right understanding about what is belief, [as if] to become a believer [in Christ] means to go to church to attend a church service… Their parents will find out [and think] 'it's only Christianity…' But if they [new believers] will be wise in this, they will keep strong influence in his family and his community, more influential than just saying, I don't care, I am going to the church. That does not work well." (306M)

This convert's early experience was of such a high tension that he simply could not continue to coexist with his relatives. But here he is advocating a reduction in this tension, and expecting this will make faith in Christ more appealing to other Muslims. This fits exactly what Stark and Finke predict, that "Sects[72] that grow will tend to reduce their tension with the sociocultural environment… [and] as sects initially lower their tension, they become more appealing to larger niches and will therefore grow" (2000, p. 205).

---

[72] Stark and Finke use the term "sect" in the sense of "New Religious Movement," i.e. a religious group that is as yet not established in a particular society. Interesting, this is exactly the same term the Central Asian governments and Islamic religious officials use to describe religious groups such as the ones being described in this thesis. There is, however, one caveat. Scholars like Stark and Finke use sect in a neutral sense, while Central Asian authorities clearly use it with heavy overtones of deviant, even illegal behavior.

5.2.3 Language of Believing

Originally I hypothesized that the three legs of this model would be the language of Joining, the language of Rejecting, and finally, the language of Continuity, assuming that continuity with natal culture would be a strong issue. However, what I found in the interviews was that while continuity certainly had value, it was expressed in different ways and was not as strong as the "language of believing." Narratives falling into this category are those which represent conversion as a decisive act of faith in Jesus/*Isa*:

> "Interviewer: Tell me about how you came to know *Isa*
>
> I grew up in a small city, way back in the mountains. I lived with my grandmother for my first five or six years. Her grandfather had been the Imam in our town. He had taught his granddaughter, my grandmother, that *Isa* was the creator of the world, that he was the only one worthy of worship, and that he would come to us whenever we prayed to him. So that is what my grandmother taught me.
>
> Interviewer: This grandmother was a Muslim?
>
> Yes. We were all Muslims, as we thought... So as a little girl I always prayed to Isa. I really cannot remember anything else about religion from those years.
>
> Interviewer: So all the years growing up you prayed to *Isa*?
>
> Yes, when I was little. I prayed to *Isa* every day. But when I got older, like in the middle school years, I stopped praying. I became like the other girls. We were thinking about boys, and reading, and other things, so I stopped praying. But I did not completely forget about *Isa*, I just became secular.

Interviewer: So what happened then?

I met my husband and he moved us to the capital city. Then things got very bad and he started drinking and doing drugs. He became angry and would beat me. Every Friday he would beat me because it was the Muslim holy day. Muslims think that women have demons and so the best way to do it is to beat them on the holy day so the demons will leave.

Interviewer: Did your husband go to the Mosque or do Namaz?

No, he was not religious at all then. [Then] In the early 90s he met some foreign missionaries in Almaty. They started to talk to him about Isa. I did not know anything about this, but he started meeting with them and reading the *Injil*. I started noticing that he was not angry all the time, he seemed nicer to me. Then one Friday he did not beat me. I was surprised. Then the next Friday he did not beat me. I was happy but I did not know why this was happening. So I asked him, 'I am very glad that you have not hit me lately, but what has made you more peaceful?' He said, 'I am reading the Bible and I realized that Jesus would not want me to hit you.'

I was very surprised! Then he told me he had met some foreigners who were teaching him about Jesus and the Bible. He had stopped drinking and doing drugs, he was much more peaceful. Now he has become such a good husband and is teaching our son to be a good man and husband.

So you see I did not learn about Isa from missionaries, I have believed in him my whole life. I have learned a lot more about *Isa* from foreigners, but they did not bring him to me." (415F)

While this narrative was almost exclusively about faith in Jesus/*Isa* it also connects with the section in chapter 4 about the metaphysical location of Jesus. Notice the shift in the participant's word choice when talking about her husband's conversion and her own faith. She said that her husband told her, "I am reading the Bible and I realized that Jesus would not want me to hit you" yet when she speaks of her own faith she exclusively uses the terms *Isa* and *Injil*. Perhaps without even being aware of it, this woman quite naturally locates her faith in *Isa* within the Muslim metaphysical world and describes her husband's faith with foreign terms, "Jesus" and the "Bible," connecting it with foreign missionaries. As if to underscore her point, she even used the English terms, "Jesus" and the "Bible," although she was speaking Russian!

And while the personal context of this narrative is unusual, for a Central Asian Muslim who had knowledge about *Isa* before any encounter with Christianity of any kind, it was not singular. This young man prefaces his own conversion by first reaching back to the faith in Isa of his father and even grandfather:

> "When I was little, my grandfather was a well-known mullah; where we lived everyone knew him and respected him. My grandfather had two wives. My father was supposed to also become a mullah. So he started counting the Namaz prayer. Before my grandfather died, he said that the truth is in *Isa*.
>
> Interviewer: He said that to your father?
>
> Yes. He said, the truth is in *Isa*. My father wondered why he said that and he started studying the Quran… It was in 1997; I was 12. At that time my father started studying; he just got into a motorcycle accident and had to stay home for a while, so he had a lot of time to read. He read the Quran, what it said about *Isa* that He was born pure, that he healed the sick, raised from the dead and casted out demons. That's all that it says about Him. Oh, it also says that *Isa* will come back. So my father didn't understand anything from the Quran and he started studying

the Bible. The Bible is very clear. So gradually he came to believe. At that time relatives came to our house, and once they found out, they began to persecute him. They said, 'What will people say? Your father was a Muslim and so are we; why are you doing this?' They called him *kafir*; they said that he was paid to believe in Jesus. My father didn't pay attention. His older brothers even brought a mullah to him who told him, 'This is not true! Who told you this?' My father answered, 'Jesus is the Son of God. God sent Him to Earth.' He told that mullah, 'Open Sura 3, ayat 45; it says that *Isa* will come back in the end of the world. No man can come back like that, so I know this is the truth'..." (418M)

Then, after several years of somewhat confused religious views he tells how the new faith of his father became his own:

"My father always told me, read *Kieli Kitap*[73] but I didn't. I had my own life with friends; even though I did not deny it as truth, but I wanted facts. My father also told me what Quran said about *Isa*, but I didn't really care. I had a friend who went to college with me and his brother was doing the *namaz*. So one day we had a discussion with them. He started telling me about Islam. I said, 'Quran says this and that' and I began to tell him about Jesus, even though I myself was not sure yet! But I told him that according to the Quran *Isa* will come back. He objected… so I started proving to him, I went home and took the Quran and asked my dad where it talked about Jesus. So I started studying it to see for myself. At first I read about *Isa*, in the *Injil*, that whoever believes in Him, the Lord will lift him up, etc. As I was reading it I cried. So as I read, I knew that even though Islam talks about Muhammad, I saw facts about Jesus there." (418M)

This next "language of believing" narrative covers many years of a young Muslim woman's sporadic interaction with the person of Jesus:

---

[73] *Keili Kitap* means "Holy Book" in Kazakh language. It is printed on the cover of the new Kazakh Bible, and is therefore used by Kazakh converts for the same.

"Interviewer: When is the first time you heard about Jesus? The very first time.

I heard about Jesus when I was eight years old, through one of my friends. She was going at that time to the Orthodox Church; she was Russian. And I remember she brought some book about Jesus, about him and his disciples. And I remember at that time I was really hungry for spiritual things…

I want to tell a story, about a time when my father was really sick. And he was close to death; he was between life and death. Like at that time I wanted to find anything, I wanted to find everything or anything that can heal my father. He was at home at that time, and when I went to the library I found this Christian magazine, and it was telling me, I don't know all it was because I was in a hurry to do my home tasks, but anyway, by end of the page I found story about Christmas, I never heard about Christmas until that time. So I found out about how Jesus was born and there was a prayer, Matt chapter 6, when he was teaching the disciples. Now I know about disciples, but at that time I didn't know what was [a] disciple. I don' know what was leading my heart, but I decided to write down this prayer on a piece of paper. So I just made this and take this prayer with me and when everybody went to sleep at my home, it was about 2 or 3 o'clock in the night, I took this prayer and started to pray… saying 'God, please do something for my father. Do something with my father. Heal my father.' I don't know how many times, how many hours I spent, maybe like two hours, I just prayed and cried and I couldn't stop to cry because I just prayed for God to heal my father. And after then I went to sleep and actually miracle happened, after several days my father was totally healed. So then, this was my first big spiritual step, to believe God, to believe Jesus. I know when I was taking this prayer and praying to God, I knew this was about Jesus.

And I knew something was interesting me in Jesus. Then I started researching more about Jesus in my life. And God healed my father totally and I knew this was a big change for my heart and mind, and I wanted to know more about Jesus now…

<u>Interviewer: So what steps did you take to try to find out more about Jesus?</u>

It was hard because we were not having any literature. We were not having anybody telling me about Jesus at that time… I remember found a little picture of Jesus that the Orthodox are using, so I am having this with me, like some kind of talisman… It was 1990 or 1992…I think I can say I was searching but nobody knows about Jesus…

And then in 1993 we had this big crusade, evangelical crusade in our town. Then I heard about Jesus, and people were inviting us to come to the stadium and everyone was announcements about how God is healing people, and of course it was taking my attention. So we had to go through this park to get there and so, and when we went through this, I saw so many people giving this New Testament, this book… And it was at this time they came and I went to the stadium twice and the preacher was asking who wanted to come to Christ… They explained what is the meaning of what it is to follow Christ…

I was the first to come to Jesus so of course I bring [converted] my sister and two younger sister and brother. So every year Christians are growing in my family. So my parents are getting very angry because now it's not only me but my sisters and brothers are Christians now. They are feeling they are losing control of us believing in Christ." (101F)

This young woman's narrative is that of conversion as a long running encounter with the person of Jesus. Time and time again this person takes center stage; first as an interesting part of Russian Orthodoxy, then as an almost magical talisman, and eventually he takes on the image of

Western revival Christianity. But from start to finish, her conversion is about believing in this evolving person of Jesus.

The following is one final narrative that is shaped strongly by the language of believing. This man's story is a significant outlier from the rest of the conversion narratives because his knowledge of Arabic and Islamic theology was a major factor in his eventual conversion to Christ. And it was this growing understanding of who Jesus/*Isa* is that shaped his narrative:

> "When I was seven years old, my father asked me to go to normal high school or to *madrassa*…, but our family was not religious, my father was just a normal person. He did not go to any mosque at that time, Soviet time he was working in the government work… And I was thinking, like, the madrassa was in another city and… it was good if I would go far from my house and then I have more freedom and it will be a good time. And then I said to my father 'I want to go to study at *madrassa*' and he said OK. And he sent me…" (102M)

Notice that his upbringing was much like that of other *russified* Muslims with a basically non-religious father who was a communist party member[74]. Yet when this young boy went to the madrassa his narrative took a huge shift. Unlike the others in this study, he became an orthodox Muslim, knowing significant Islamic theological content *prior* to his conversion to Christ. Upon return home for a visit, he found out that his older sister had converted to Christ, so he decided to find what the Quran had to say about *Isa*:

> "But later I was looking to see what the Quran has to say about *Isa*, and in Arabic it says this is '*Hazereti Isa*' and for me this was interesting. What is the meaning

---

[74] In the interview he calls his father a "government worker," but we can take this to mean that he was probably a Communist party member since government jobs were reserved for them.

of this word '*hazereti*'? *Hazereti* means like sinless. The sinless. Then I asked myself, Islam teaches that all the prophets were very good persons but they have sin. Their level is higher than other people but they have sin. The Quran says that Muhammed has sin... in the original Quran it says *hazereti, hazereti,* everywhere it says *hazereti* Isa... over and over, "Jesus the sinless." And then it is very logical, if the Quran and many other places say like only Allah has no sin, but all the people have sin, even prophets...

[It is] very clear in the Quran that all the prophets have sin. But only God is sinless. But if only Allah is sinless why do people say *hazereti Isa*? Then also the Quran recognizes that Jesus is sinless. And then that was very powerful for me.

...Then from the prophet level they have taken him up. They are saying that he is higher, they are taking him above. This is because 'Allah' is God the one. Because this is making *Isa* like God, like Allah... Anyway for me it was interesting the Quran saying about *Isa* is *hazereti*, and I started thinking that Jesus is like different than Muhammad, and I didn't find another book about him, a bibliography. But all the gospels says about him how he was born and how he died." (102M)

So while this narrative was certainly an outlier in some ways, not everything in his story is unusual. Like many of the others, his conversion is clearly presented as a turn to embrace belief in the person of Jesus/*Isa*.

Eminent scholar of religious conversion, Lewis Rambo, has argued that an encounter with the holy and transcendent constitutes both the source and goal of conversion (1993, pp 17-18). Study participants expressed this, a personal encounter with a transcendent being, Jesus/*Isa* through the "language of believing." But conversion is also embedded in social processes; and we saw that people tell stories which account for that as well. We called these stories the languages of "joining" and "rejecting." The fact that the major themes of these narratives significantly varied is a reminder that Christianity is still in its infancy in Central Asia, at least as a faith choice for people from traditionally Muslim ethnicities. Mary and Van Reidhead describe how the range of possible narrative categories contracts as religions become more entrenched, but at the same time this is counterproductive. Converts need to be able to fully and freely express their conversion, in categories that fit their experience, in order to fully integrate into their new faith (2003). Based on the analysis of the three languages of conversion, it would seem that these converts from Islam are well integrated into their new faith.

5.3 Conversion as a non-Linear Movement

Many theories project the idea that conversion is a singular act or movement. It is often presented as a process such as "switching" (Sherkat and Wilson 1995; Radford 2011; Hefner 1998), a movement from one "place" to another. Although complex models which account for stages or steps, they still present the picture of movement toward a fixed goal, the new faith. The researcher comes across as the omniscient narrator of someone else's story who knows where the convert is going, thus presents conversion as an almost linear movement. Perhaps it is just me and my background in mechanics, but this thinking, "switching" in particular, implies that a person's belief system moved like a light switch, from one contact point to another—as if there are only two positions. This may not be the intention of the authors, but the imagery is hard to ignore. Switches are things that move between poles, usually in a straight line, a binary movement from one to the other. Yet the image of a straight line hardly describes the way that conversion played out for those who participated in this study; linear movement cannot explain many of the accounts of conversion which I encountered. Movement is clearly in view, but it is seldom anything like a crisp switch between poles.

Finding 7: Conversion in Central Asia is not usually a singular move, as if going from one socio-religious 'place' to another directly. It is often a series of movements, some of which are better classified as 'sideways movement' or even a partial return toward one's natal socio-religious background.

Rather than a "once-and-done" affair, participants often described their conversion more like a continuing process. That is, the initial conversion experience, no matter how dramatic the initial turning, was sometimes only the first of several related spiritual turns.

> "I became a believer in 1996… My mother [had become] became a believer through our neighbor… she told me about *Isa* and that she became a believer. She didn't say anything else, she didn't say 'You need to accept Him' or anything like that. We were just talking as we worked. But I kept thinking about it all day long, about Jesus saving us from our sin… But I couldn't sleep that night, and I went and took the Bible and I began to read and something began to happen inside me. I started crying. My grandmother was lying there, sleeping with me, and she asked, 'Why are you not sleeping? What are you doing?' In one paper it said 'If you want to believe, say this prayer'. So I cried and said that on my own, so that's how I became a believer… Two years later I went to church in the capital city and stayed there." (301F)

Her conversion started out as a fairly low key affair through the agency of a couple of Russian schoolmates and her mother. Soon she was a stable member of a Baptist church in the capital city. There she meets another young believer, the man who would later become her husband. There they began the slow process of enculturating into the Baptist church culture:

> "My husband used to be a musician, he is from up in the mountains, one of the first [Kyrgyz] believers. He used to work at a cultural center there, and did it well. When he came here to the capital and when he went to the church, everyone there were Russian. He said, 'everyone around had blond hair, and I was the only black man among them!' At that time we went to a Baptist church and he was told that it was a sin to sing secular songs [so] he burned the tape of his band with songs that was even used on TV… All of his friends were upset and left him because that was their future, they could be famous now if they promoted those songs." (301F)

Eventually the young bride and groom chose to make a public statement, a radical break with the past, making it clear to their friends and family that they were now Christians. They went so far as to ask their Korean missionary pastors to speak at the event.

> "In 2003 my husband and I were married and we invited everyone to a café but we talked about Jesus and said that we were Christian. Our preachers preached there…" (301F)

But the result was not what they were expecting:

> "We lost all of our relatives after our wedding in 2003. Only believers stayed with us. We thought we did it for the non-believers but in actuality we did it for the Christians. Our non-Christian relatives began to leave right in the middle of the wedding." (301F)

The reasons for this rejection were not really persecution; rather it was the strangeness of their new religion:

"Kyrgyz have different weddings than Christians, and we don't wear white gloves like Koreans do. That different culture scares Kyrgyz people… [And] our internal Christian language was quite bad. It's our own 'church' language. So when they were blessing us, to our relatives it was like people spoke some unknown language even though they spoke Kyrgyz. But they could not understand and thought of us as crazy people. So a group of relatives went to another café and celebrated without us. My friends they were in shock. They were wondering why I would go there [to the church]; they thought that only weak and foolish people go there. At that time the Baptist church gave out humanitarian aid to people with financial difficulties. So they thought that only poor people go to church to ask for help." (301F)

They started out believing that being faithful members of a Baptist church was how someone expressed their faith in Christ. They were so committed to that group and that identity that they eventually became completely detached from their relatives and their culture.

"When my husband's father died, we realized that we didn't know any of the relatives, we were out of contact with them for so long! We were so lost; we didn't know what to do! My husband was the oldest but he had no idea what to do, so the brother after him took the responsibility because he knew more than my husband… There were five or six Kyrgyz believers from our church but they also didn't know what to do, it was like we all came from a different culture. So that was our first cultural shock. So after this, all of his relatives said, 'You are like the head [of the family] now, so you must contact all relatives to inform them of family events; you must know when we have celebrations and to know what rituals to do.' They asked, 'Or do you not want to do that?' My husband felt so bad about it! Of course we did what we could do, but we were so far from it… So that made us think - how did we come to this? We felt like we lost our identity, we were not Kyrgyz any longer, but we didn't know what we were. So it made us think, what do we do? …

Until 2006 I had a conviction to tell everyone that I was a Christian. Then later, as life changed and as I grew up, now I never call myself a Christian among my own people. Same with my husband… So now we have a small group where four, five, or six families come together to talk, eat and share. We take turns at whose house we meet. We don't say, 'Let's worship God!' but if someone says, 'please sing something, you are a musician,' my husband might sing a couple songs about life and about God who created us, etc. But this is more effective for us…" (301F)

This conversion narrative started out as a simple, even dramatic switch to a Baptist church, but eventually it led down a much longer path back toward experimentation with ways of being both a follower of Christ and Kyrgyz, something that was for all practical purposes impossible while aligned with the missionaries and their expressions of faith.

Next we will revisit an interview that we examined earlier as an example of the language of joining. This young man began his interest in Christ desperately wanting to be part of the *JanSport* backpack crowd, like the international college students he saw at a particular church, in his own words a "very western style" church:

"And I really liked it. And since I joined an American organization I wanted to improve my English. I wanted to listen to western music; I wanted to be just like these people. Probably this was also [because] I was a provincial boy—I wanted to be like these others. Because the young people at church had many things like westerners—*JanSport* backpacks[75] and speaking English to the expat people, I was like, I also wanted to do this, to talk to people like this… At that time in my

---

[75] *JanSport* was at that time a very popular American brand, similar to *Nike* or *Adidas*.

life I didn't have many friends, I was introverted person, very reserved. And here I met people who were very interested in my life. They would invite me places. I felt esteemed valued. And I wanted more...I remember I wanted a *JanSport* back pack!" (201M)

A perfect example of a self-described cultural marginal for whom converting the Christ was a means of social mobility, mobility up and out of his natal culture. But later, he left the capital city and pursued his ex-wife back home. After they remarried they moved to her home village:

> "Interviewer: How did you explain yourself to your wife's family? Did you talk overtly about your identity?
>
> I usually say that I am a believer in *Isa Masah*. And I openly say that I read the *Injil*. People would say behind me that I was a betrayer of Islam. But people still call me *Kafir*... I used to tell people the term 'Christian,' but that was in the past... [Now]I try to be careful in how I do things. For example, praying after the food not before. Praying in Islamic way, saying *Ameen*... I purposefully choose not to do some things." (201M)

Moving from the capital city back home to a provincial city, and then to a village can also be seen as analogous to this man's non-linear conversion experience. In the capital he sought to identify with the in crowd, but time, maturity, and the pressures of living under closer scrutiny in his wife's home village brought about another change. Just like in the story above, his initial conversion was both to Christ and *away from his culture*. And although for perhaps different reasons, like the woman in the first narrative, he too eventually took steps back toward his natal culture and society.

Building on the work of Donald Gelpi, a Jesuit theologian, Lewis Rambo suggests that genuine conversion requires the person to develop and grow beyond an exclusively personal conversion and into some kind of active engagement with social structures and cultural institutions. He calls this "the difference between initial and ongoing conversion" (1993, p. 147). In both of the narratives above, and several others like them in the data set, we see exactly the kind of "ongoing" conversion that Rambo predicted. If converts are to continue to live in any way as part of their natal culture, they must come to some sense of peace with it. Notice in the first narrative that no adjustment took place as long as the convert was living fully immersed in the culture of the church. But when life cycles reasserted themselves at the death of her father-in-law, the stage was set for a choice. After the funeral, the brothers-in-law brought the issue to a head with her husband, "You are like the head [of the family] now, so you must contact all relatives to inform them of family events; you must know when we have celebrations and to know what rituals to do." They asked, "Or do you not want to do that?"

However, a word of caution is in order here. It would be easy to frame this exclusively in modern anthropological construct and forget that this phenomenon is neither new, nor particular to post-Soviet Central Asia. It reflects an ancient and deep impulse in the Christian faith, dating at least back to the time of Augustine of Canterbury (circa the first half of the 6th Century). Christian faith has "subjected the principal of transmission to the dynamics of reception and adaptation… [and] the primacy of indigenous appropriation" (Sanneh 2008, p. 47). The non-linear movement in these conversion narratives are simply the result of this "indigenous appropriation."

Chapter 6 - Conclusions

6.1 The Research Question Revisited

In order to draw final conclusions from this research and consider its significance, we must briefly review the purposes of this study. This can be expressed in one succinct research question:

<u>What do the conversion narratives of Muslim converts to Christ in post-Soviet Central Asia tell us about the way they understand their conversion, the contextual influences on their conversions, and the nature of religious conversion itself?</u>

There are three aspects to this research question: 1) emic understandings of conversion, 2) contextual factors, and 3) the ontology of religious conversion. Although chapters four and five did not flow in this same order, I will follow the order of the original research question as I explore the following conclusions.

Emic Understandings of Conversion

Explaining an emic perspective is one of the most daunting challenges faced by the ethnographer or anthropologist. Not only does this require slipping into the worldview of people who may be very different, but also the researcher must then make those alien thoughts intelligible to his own audience. There is always a danger of leaving the research hanging at either extreme: staying so closely to the words of the field participants that the systems of meaning remain enigmatic, or so overanalyzing them that they sound as if they were uttered by the neighbor next door.

There were two primary dimensions to the emic perspective developed in the interviews, and they related to Findings two and six:

Finding 2: For many Central Asian Muslims, Jesus is inaccessible until he, as *Isa*, enters into their culturally-constructed metaphysical landscape. The primary example of this linguistic phenomenon is the change of the Russian religious figure *Yesus Christos* into *Isa Masih*.

Finding 6: Conversion narratives often have major, overarching themes—or "languages" through which they are told. For Central Asian Muslims converting to Christ, three of these were most common: the language of joining, the language of rejecting, and the language of believing.

Although at first glance these two findings seem disconnected, they share an important commonality, the importance of speech for constructing reality. Obviously, the person named Jesus, who is portrayed in the pages of the New Testament, is the same whether he is spoken of using his Russian name, *Yesus Christos*, or the one derived from Quranic material, *Isa Masih*. However, the perception about which culture Jesus/*Isa* belongs to changes dramatically with word usage, thus illustrating the way linguistics can alter narrative reality. This was further illustrated as some participants created themes of discourse which revealed their own understanding of their conversion: the language of joining, the language of rejecting, and the language of believing. Taken together, these two linguistic constructions offer significant depth of insight into the emic perspective that my research question sought to find.

Contextual Factors of Central Asian Conversions

The second aspect of the original research question that I would address has to do with context; and this resulted in occupying the lion's share of this study. Without a doubt, *Russification* emerged as the meta-context of the conversions in this study. I would go so far as to say that it is impossible to overstate the importance of this issue. From the historical overview in chapter one, to the repeated appearances of Russian Christians as agents of religious change in chapter four, *Russification* had a huge impact on these conversion narratives. Three of the formal findings in this study, numbers one, three, and four, pertain to *Russification*, with the first finding being in some ways the fountainhead of the others.

Finding 1: As it concerns conversion to Christ, the impact of Russian culture on Central Asian Muslims is best thought of as a continuum, with Russification on one end and *Sovietization* at the other.

Finding 3: A significant factor in the conversions of Central Asian Muslims is the legacy of Soviet era efforts to increase literacy. This laid the groundwork for the textual nature of Protestant Christianity which Muslims later encountered.

Finding 4: The primary agents of Muslim conversions in Central Asia were usually local Russian Christians and other former Muslims-turned-evangelists. Foreign missionaries mostly played a secondary role, if any at all.

The long-term interaction between Russians and Central Asian Muslims is the key to understanding how these conversions to Christ are different from those that might take place in other countries, such as Turkey or Libya. As I have contended throughout this thesis, context is critical, because people not only convert *to*, they also convert *from*. Living in close proximity to, and in deep social interaction with Russians brought about profound changes in the lives of Central Asian Muslims. For some, it was a worldview transformation, as evidenced by deep levels of psychological *Russification,* that framed their openness to conversion. For others, it was the Soviet push for Russian literacy, which moved the lotus of authority from tradition to text, thus laying the groundwork for the Protestant version of Christianity. However, the most significant element was simply that by studying, working, or simply living in close proximity to Russians, Muslims inevitably encountered Russian Christians, thus giving rise to effective cross-cultural proselytism. In short, the context of the conversions in this study was thoroughly framed by the Russian cultural milieu, without which they would have been very different.

Ontology of Religious Conversion

This final aspect of the original research question requires us to step back from the particulars and consider the larger picture, conversion itself. This issue is addressed by Finding numbers five and seven, which point to issues that clearly reach beyond the limits of this study.

<u>Finding 5</u>: Within the metaphor of "spiritual migration," the factors that influence conversions to Christ in Central Asia can be categorized within the push/pull framework common to human migration studies.

<u>Finding 7</u>: Conversion in Central Asian is not usually a singular move, as if going directly from one socio-religious 'place' to another. It is often a series of non-linear movements constituting something closer to a 'continuous conversion.'

Conversion is a movement through metaphysical space. Whether we conceptualize it as a "spiritual migration" or as a series of non-linear steps, the study participants painted pictures of conversion that were much closer to a *journey* than to a *decision*. Considering the prevalence of the idea, "conversion as movement" reflects part of the intrinsic ontology of what it means for a person to turn from and turn to.

6.2 Contributions

This study makes at least three significant contributions to the field of religious studies in general, and conversion studies in particular:

Establishing context as a primary issue in conversion

In bringing together the deeply personal (self-constructed narratives) and broadly sociological (*Russification*), I have demonstrated the importance of context to religious conversion. Many other studies have inadvertently hinted at this matter, but this study has forged a clear and compelling link between religious/historical context and the way people experience conversion. This in turn indicates that the anthropological study of conversion, that which is grounded in human contexts, should be given precedence over psychological and theological speculations of the same.

Showing a fuller picture of the nature of Russification.

One of the most significant gaps in the literature on Central Asia is a clear understanding of *Russification.* This involves all things concrete, but particularly how it affected interreligious dialogue. Perhaps the irreligious nature of the Soviet state blinded scholars to the potential release of pent-up religious fervor displayed by Russian Christians at the end of the Soviet era. This study offers a completely different metric by which to understand the degree and nature of *Russification* and its impact on the peoples of Central Asia. In particular, I have shown that *Russification* directly impacted at least two aspects of religious change in Central Asia. First, it facilitated ethnic Russian Christians' becoming effective conversion agents among *russified* Muslims. Secondly, this study illustrated the way Soviet literacy efforts shifted the locus of religious authority from traditional sources to textual ones, thus opening the way for the Protestant emphasis on the Bible as the source of faith and behavior, as opposed to traditional community sources of authority that the people knew in Central Asian *islam.*

The use of a push-pull framework of migration studies for conversion studies.

One of the weaknesses of the literature on conversion is that it lacks a field-research friendly framework through which to study and discuss factors of conversion. By appropriating the migration metaphor, particularly the idea of push-pull factors, this study offers students of conversion a simple structure with which to work. Not so much as a point for further research, but my start in this area could be refined into a convenient heuristic. Such an investigative model would be particularly help for undergraduate students who are not yet ready to handle more challenging aspects of qualitative studies such as Grounded Theory development.

6.3 Directions for Further Research

A good research project raises as many questions as it answers, perhaps even more. That is the nature of empirical investigation; the more we know about something, the more questions we know to ask. This project was no different. The depth of the research raised many questions and ideas that the focus of my research question did not allow me to explore. Below are a few related research ideas that would be worthy of further exploration;

1. Study of intensification conversions to orthodox Islam.

    Besides conversion to Christ, post-Soviet Central Asia has undoubtedly also seen "intensification conversions," i.e. Muslims who "converted" from the localized *islam* prevalent in the region, to universal, orthodox Islam. What has been the nature and shape of these conversions, and how did the post-Soviet context impact those?

2. A quantitative study to understand the relative weight of push-pull factors in conversion.

    Our discussion in this thesis about push-pull factors in conversion is little more than an opening salvo in what should be a much larger investigation. It is not enough to know that some factors push a person away from the natal religion while others pull them toward a new faith. The picture would be much more complete with a follow-up quantitative study to determine the relative weight of these factors.

3. <u>Investigation into previous generations' knowledge of Jesus/*Isa*.</u>

    Some of the study participants gave tantalizing glimpses of knowledge about Jesus/*Isa* that was passed down to them from their elders. As if to drive this point home, in one narrative we considered, this mysterious, non-Quranic Jesus/*Isa* forms the core of the narrative. Are these the result of early, undocumented Christian/Muslim interactions on the Russian frontier? Or might they be faint echoes of the Syriatic church, which once played a significant role in Central Asia? The answer to these questions should be of great interest to anyone interested in the religious history of Central Asia.

6.4 Personal Reflections

As explained in the introduction to this study, my family and I previously lived and worked in post-Soviet Central Asia for more than ten years. Thus, despite a commitment to letting the data speak for itself via a Grounded Theory approach, I must admit that I felt I already knew a great deal about this region and the Muslims who converted to Christ there. Now, looking back, I realize how very little I knew at that time, and how much there is *still* to be learned. Whenever the intangibles of personal religious faith intersect with the complexities of a living social context, the result is a fascinating human kaleidoscope. And while the experience was personally and academically enriching to me, I sincerely hope the people I interviewed were also benefited by their participation in this study; for the story of Muslim conversions to Christ in post-Soviet Central Asia is truly theirs, not mine.

Works Cited

Adler, H.E. (1946). "Turkistan in Transition." *The Geographic Journal.* Vol. 107, No. 5/6 (May-Jun), pp. 230-235.

Alexander, Gary T. (1980) William James, the Sick Soul, and the Negative Dimensions of Consciousness. *Journal of the American Academy of Religion*, Vol. 48, No. 2, pp. 191-205.

Anderson, Barbara A. and Brian D. Silver. (1983). Estimating Russification of Ethnic Identity Among Non-Russians in the USSR. *Demography.* Vol. 20, No. 4 (Nov), pp. 461-489.

Asad, Talal. (1996). "Comments on Conversion" in *Conversion to Modernities: The Globalization of Christianity.* Peter Van der Veer, editor. New York: Routledge.

Aspaturian, Vernon V. (1968). "The non-Russian nationalities," in *Prospects for Soviet Society.* New York: Praeger. Allen Kassof ed.. A Publication of the Council on Foreign Relations. Pp 143-198.

Atkin, Muriel. (1992). "Religious, National, and Other Identities in Central Asia" in *Muslims in Central Asia: Expressions of Identity and Change.* Jo-Ann Gross ed. Durham, N.C.: Duke University Press.

Austin-Broos, Diane. (2003). Introduction. In Andrew Buckser and Stephen D. Glasier eds. *The Anthropology of Conversion.* New York: Rowman & Littlefield Publishers.

Barnett, Jens. (2008). *Conversion's Consequences: Identity, Belonging, and Hybridity amongst Muslim Followers of Christ in the Kingdom of Jordan.* Coming to Faith Conference II. February 2010. London.

Barro, Robert J., Jason Hwang, and Rachel M. McCleary. (n.d.). *Religious Converions in 40 Countries.* Cornerstone Research Papers, Harvard University.

Bateson, C. Daniel, Patricia Schoenrade, and W. Larry Ventis. 1993. *Religion and the Individual.* New York: Oxford University Press.

Becker, Seymour. (1968) *Russia's Protectorates in Central Asia.* Cambridge, Mass: Harvard University Press.

Bennigsen, Alexandre. (1969). Colonization and Decolonization in the Soviet Union. In *Journal of Contemorary History.* Vol. 4, No. 1, (Jan. 1969), pp. 141-151

Bielefeldt, Heiner. (1995). "Muslim Voices in the Human Rights Debate, *Human Rights Quarterly.* Vol. 17, No. 4 (Nov), pp. 587-617.

Bjorkman, W. (1990). Kafir. In: C.E. Bosworth, E. van Donzel, B. Lewis and Ch. Phellat (eds) *Encyclopaedia of Islam.* New Edition. Vol. 4 IRAN-KHA. Leiden: E.J. Brill.

Blanchard, Dallas A. (1994). Book review. "Understanding Religious Conversion by Lewis Rambo". *Contemporary Sociology.* Vol 23, No. 5 (Sept). 737-738.

Bloomberg, Linda Dale, Marie Volpe. (2008). *Completing Your Qualitative Dissertation: A Roadmap from Beginning to End.* London: Sage Publications.

Boote, David N. and Penny Beile. (2005). Scholars before Researchers: On the Centrality of the Dissertation Literature Review in Research Preparation. *Educational Researcher.* Vol. 34, No. 6 (Aug – Sept), pp. 3-15.

Bremmer, Jan N., Wout J. van Bekkum, and Arie L. Molendijk. (2006). *Paradigm, Poetics, and Politics of Conversion.* Leuven: Peeters.

Bruner, Jerome. (1991). The Narrative Construction of Reality. *Critical Inquiry*, Vol. 18, No. 1 (Autumn, 1991), pp. 1-21. Accessed 03/08/2011 at stable URL <http://www.jstor.org/stable/1343711>.

Buckser, Andrew and Stephen D. Glazier. (2003). *The Anthropology of Religious Conversion.* Oxford: Rowman & Littlefield Publishers.

Butler-Kesber, Lynn, et al. (2003). "Insight and Voice: Artful Analysis in Qualitative Inquiry". *Arts and Learning Research.* Vol. 19, No. 1 (2002-2003), pp. 127-165.

Buton-Page, J. (1993). Namaz. In: C.E. Bosworth, E. van Donzel, B. Lewis and Ch. Phellat (eds) *Encyclopaedia of Islam.* New Edition. Vol. 7 MIF-NAZ. Leiden: E.J. Brill.

Cassell, Manuel. (1997). *The Power of Identity.* Oxford: Blackwell Publishers.

Clark, Charles E. (1995). "Literacy and Labor: The Russian Literacy Campaign within the Trade Unions, 1923-27." *Europe-Asia Studies.* Vol. 47, No 8. Pp. 1327-1341. Accessed on Feb. 8, 2014 at stable URL <http://www.jstor.org/stable/153300>.

Clark, William. (2009). Networks of Faith in Kazkahstan. In Mathijs Pelkmans ed. *Conversion After Socialism: Disruptions, Modernisms, and Technologies of Faith in the Former Soviet Union.* New York: Berghahn.

Connelly, Michael F., and D. Jean Clandinin. (1990). Stories of Experience and Narrative Inquiry. In *Educational Researcher.* Vol. 19, No. 5 (Jun-Jul), pp. 2-14. Accessed on July 10, 2013 at stable URL <http://www.jstor.org/stable/1176100>.

_____. (2006). Narrative Inquiry. In J. Green, G. Camilli, & P. Elmore (Eds.), *Handbook of Complementary Methods in Education Research* (pp. 375-385). Mahwah, NJ: Lawrence Erlbaum.

Darden, Keith and Anna Gryzmala-Busse. (2006). "The Great Divide: Literacy, Nationalism, and the Communist Collapse." *World Politics.* Vol. 59, No. 1 (Oct., 2006), pp. 83-115. Accessed on Feb. 8, 2014 at stable URL <http://www.jstor.org/stable/40060156>.

Datta, Pranati. (2004). "Push-Pull Factors of Undocumented Migration from Bangladesh to West Bengal: A Perception Study." *The Qualitative Report.* Vol. 9, No. 2 (June 2004), pp. 335-358. Accessed on Feb. 8, 2014 at stable <URL http://www.nova.edu/ssss/QR/QR9-2/datta.pdf>.

Dickens, Mark. (2001). *Nestorian Christianity in Central Asia.* Accessed May 31, 2013 at stable URL < http://www.oxuscom.com/Nestorian_Christianity_in_CA.pdf >

Dittes, James. (1973). "Beyond William James" in *Essays in the Scientific Study of Religion,* Charles Y. Glock and Phillip E. Hammond, eds. Pp. 291-354. New York: Harper and Row, Torchbook edition.

Dufault-Hunter, Erin Elizabeth. (2005). *Personal Transformation and Religious Faith: A Narrative Approach to Conversion.* A Dissertation Presented to the Faculty of the Graduate School University of Southern California. In Partial Fulfillment of the Requirements for the Degree Doctor of Philosophy (Religion).

Dunn, Ethel and Stephan P. Dunn. (1964). Religion as an Instrument of Culture Change: The Problem of the Sects in the Soviet Union. *Slavic Review,* Vol. 23, No. 3 (Sep., 1964), pp. 459-478. Accessed July 09, 2012 at stable URL < http://www.jstor.org/stable/2492684 >.

Durkheim, Emile. (2008). *The Elementary Forms of Religious Life.* (Unabridged version). New York: Oxford University Press.

Eickelman, Dale E. (1993). *Russia's Muslim Frontiers: New Directions in Cross-Cultural Analysis.* Bloomington IN: Indiana University Press.

el-Zien, Abdul Hamid. (1977). "Beyond Ideology and Theology: The Search for the Anthropology of Islam." *Annual Review of Anthropology.* Vol. 6, pp. 227-254.

Evens-Pritchard, EE. (1965). *Theories of Primitive Religion.* Oxford: Clarendon Press.

Fouberg, Erin H., Alexander B. Murphy and H.J. de Blij. (2012). *Human Geography: People, Place, and Culture.* 10th edition. New York: Wiley.

Freeman, Linton C., A. Kimball Romney, and Sue C. Freeman. (1987). "Cognitive Structure and Informant Accuracy." *American Anthropologist, New Series.* Vol. 89, No. 2 (Jan, 1987), pp. 310-325. Accessed on October 14, 2013 at stable URL <http://www.jstor.org/stable/677757>.

Freeman, Melissa, Kathleen de Marrais, Judith Preissle, Kathryn Roulston, and Elizabeth A. St Pierre. (2007). "Standards of Evidence in Qualitative Research." *Educational Researcher.* Vol. 36, No. 1 (Jan-Feb), pp. 25-32. Accessed October 15, 2013 at stable URL <http://jstor.org.stable/4621065>.

Geertz, Clifford. (1968). *Islam Observed.* New Haven, CN: Yale University Press.

Glaser, Barney G. (2003). *The Grounded Theory Perspective II. Description's Remodeling of Grounded Theory Methodology.* Mill Valley, CA: Sociology Press.s

Glaser, Barney G. and Anselm L. Strauss. (1967). *The Discovery of Grounded Theory.* Chicago: Aldine Publishing.

Gooren, Henri. (2007). "Reassessing Conventional Approaches to Conversion" in *Journal for the Scientific Study of Religion. Vol. 46, No. 3. Pp. 337-353.*

Greenlee, David. (1996). *Christian Conversion From Islam.* A Dissertation submitted in partial fulfillment of the requirements for the degree of Doctor of Philosophy in Intercultural Studies at Trinity International University. Deerfield IL.

_____. (2005). *From the Straight Path to the Narrow Way.* Milton Keynes: Authentic Media.

Guba, Egon G. and Yvonna S. Lincoln. (1989). *Fourth Generation Evaluation.* Newburry Park, CA: Sage Publications.

Harran, Marilyn. (1983). *Luther on Conversion.* Ithaca, NY: Cornell University Press.

Hefner, R.W. (1993). *Conversion to Christianity.* Los Angeles: University of California Press.

_____ (1998). "Multiple Modernities: Christianity, Islam, and Hinduism in a Globalizing Age." *Annual Review of Anthropology,* Vol. 27 (1998), pp 83-104. Accessed February 13, 2014 at stable URL < http://www.jstor.org/stable/223364>.

Hiebert, Paul G. (1983). "The Category 'Christian' in the Mission Task," *International Review of Mission*, 72:287, Jul-1983, pp 421-427.

Hiro, Dilip. (1994). *Between Marx and Muhammad: The Changing Face of Central Asia.* New York: HarperCollins.

Hussan A. (2004). *Interview with author.* Almaty, Kazakhstan.

Isichei, Elizabeth. (1970). "Seven Varieties of Ambiguity: Some Patterns of Igbo Response to Christian Mission." *Journal of Religion in Africa.* Vol 3. 209-27.

James, William. *The Varieties of Religious Experience: A Study in Human Nature.* New York: Macmillan, 1961.

Jensen, Jeppe, Sinding. (2003). *The Study of Religion in a New Key.* Langelandsgade: Aarhus University Press.

Juvaini, 'Ala-ad-Din "Ata Malik. (1958) *The History of World Conquerers. Vol. 2.* Translated from the text of Mirza Muhammad Qazvini by J.A. Boyle. Cambridge: unknown.

Kaganovsky, Lilya. (2004). "How the Soviet Man was (Un)Made." *Slavic Review.* Vol. 63, No. 3 (Autumn, 2004), pp. 577-596.

Kane, Danielle, and Jung Mee Park. (2009). "The Puzzle of Korean Christianity." *American Journal of Sociology.* Vol. 115, No. 2 (Sept. 2009), pp. 365-404.

Khalid, Adeeb. (2007). *Islam After Communism: Religion and Politics in Central Asia.* Berkley: University of California Press.

Killingray, David. African Missionary Activity at Home and Overseas, [Lecture]. Oxford Centre for Missions Studies, 15 March 2005.

Kim, S.I. (2008). "Conversion" in *Global Dictionary of Theology.* William A. Dyrness and Veli-Mattie Karkkainen, eds. Downers Grove, IL: Intervarsity Press.

Kimmage, Daniel. (2005). *Central Asia: Jadidism—Old Tradition of Renewal.* Radio Free Europe/Radio Liberty, Central Asia Report. Vol. 5, No. 30, 11 Aug. 2005.

Kraft, Kathryn A. (2007). *Community and Identity Among Arabs of a Muslim Background who Choose to Follow A Christian Faith.* A dissertation submitted to the University of Bristol in accordance with the requirements of the degree of Doctor of Philosophy in the Faculty of Social Sciences and Law.

Kuhn, Thomas S. (1996). *The Structure of Scientific Revolutions.* Chicago: The University of Chicago Press.

Kyrgizmanov, S. (2005). *Interview with author.* Almaty, Kazakhstan.

Lambek, Michael. (2002). "Introduction" in *A Reader in the Anthropology of Religion.* Michael Lambek ed. Oxford: Blackwell.

Larossa, Ralph, Linda A. Bennett, and Richard J. Gelles. (1981). "Ethical Dilemmas in Qualitative Family Research." *Journal of Marriage and Family.* Vol. 43, No. 2 (May, 1981), pp. 303-313. Accessed October 14, 2013 at stable URL <http://jstor.org/stable/351382>.

Laruelle, Marlene. (2008). "The Concept of Ethnogenesis in Central Asia" in *Kritka: Explorations in Russian and Eurasian History.* Vol. 9. No. 1. (Winter, new series). Pp. 169-188.

Latourette, Kenneth Scott. (2003). *A History of Christianity: Beginnings to 1500.* Fifth edition. Peabody, MA: Prince Press. Lee, Raymond M. (1993). *Doing Research on Sensitive Topics.* London: Sage Publications.

LeCompte, Margaret D. and Jean J. Schensul. (1999). *Analyzing & Interpreting Ethnographic Data.* Walnut Creek CO: AltaMira Press.

Levy-Bruhl, Lucien. (1923). *Primitive Mentality.* New York: Macmillan.

Lieblich, Amia, Rivka Tuval-Machiach, and Tamar Zilber. (1998). *Narrative Research: Reading, Analysis, and Interpretation.* Applied Social Research Methods Series Volume 47. Thousand Oaks, CA: Sage Publications.

Liu, Morgan. (2011). Central Asia in the Post-Cold War World. *Annual Review of Anthropology* [Online]. 40 (Prepublication manuscript, June 2011).

Loftand, John and Normon Skonovd. (1981). "Conversion Motifs" in *Journal of the Scientific Study of Religion.* Vol. 20, No. 4. pp. 373-385.

Lofland, John and Rodney Stark. (1965). "Becoming a World-Saver: A Theory of Conversion to a Deviant Perspective" in *American Sociological Review*, Vol. 30, No. 6 (Dec). pp. 862-75.

Lohmann, Roger. (2003). "Turning in the Belly: Insights on Religious Conversion from New Guinea Gut Feelings" in *The Anthropology of Religious Conversion* Andrew Buckser and Stephen D. Glazier eds. Boulder CO: Rowman & Littlefield Publishers.

Louw, Maria Elizabeth. (2007). *Everyday Islam in Post-Soviet Central Asia.* New York: Routledge.

Martin, Terry. *The Affirmative Action Empire: Nations and Nationalism in the Soviet Union, 1923-1999.* Ithaca, NY: Cornell University Press, 2001.

Masud, Mohammad, Khalid. (1993). "The Limits of 'Expert' Knowledge" in *Russia's Muslim Frontiers.* Dale F. Eickelman editor. Bloomington IN: Indiana University Press.

McBrien, Julie, and Mathijs Pelkmans. (2008). "Turning Marx on his Head: Missionaries, 'Extremists' and Archaic Secularists in Post-Soviet Kyrgyzstan" in *Critique of Anthropology.* Vol. 28(1), pp. 87-103.

Miles M.B. and Huberman, A.M. (1994). *Qualitative Data Analysis: An Expanded Sourcebook* (2nd ed.). Thousand Oaks: Sage.

Moffett, Samuel Hugh. (2009). *A History of Christianity in Asia Volume I: Beginnings to 1500.* Mary Knoll, NY: Orbis Books.

Murphy, Christopher. (1992). Abdullah Qadiry and the Bolsheviks: From Reform to Revolution. In *Muslims in Central Asia: Expressions of Identity and Change.* Jo-Ann Gross Ed. Durham, NC: Duke University Press.

Myer, Will. (2012). *Islam and Colonialism: Western Perspectives on Soviet Asia.* New York: Routledge.

Malashenko, Alexei, (1993). "Islam and Communism: The Experience of Coexistence" in *Russia's Muslim Frontiers.* Dale Eickelman Ed. Bloomington: Indiana University Press.

Morrison, Karl, F. (1992). *Understanding Conversion.* Charlottesville, VA: University Press of Virginia.

Morrison, Toni. (1993). *Playing in the Dark: Whiteness and the Literary Imagination.* New York: Random House.

Munis, Sher Muhammad, and Huhammad Riza Agai. (cira 1928). *F-daws al-Iqbal (The Paradise of Felicity).* Translated in 1988 by Yuri Bregel. Leiden: unknown.

Nock, Arthur Darby. (1933). *Conversion: The Old and the New in Religion from Alexander the Great to Augustine of Hippo.* London: Oxford University Press.

Nations Online Project. (2013). Central Asia. Scale 1:17,000,000. Lambert Conformal Conical Projection. Central Asia. Accessed on July 2, 2013 at stable URL <http://www.nationsonline.org/maps/Central-Asia-Map.jpg>.

Nielsen, Donald, A. (1998). "Theory" in *Encyclopedia of Religion and Society* (Web version), William Swatos editor in chief. Walnut Creek, CA: AltaMira Press. Accessed on June 25, 2012 at stable URL <http://hirr.hartsem.edu/ency/Theory.htm>.

Noor, O'Neill Borbieva. (2012). Foreign faiths and national renewal: Christian conversion among Kyrgyz youth. *Culture and Religion: An Interdisciplinary Journal.* Vol. 13, No. 1, pp. 41-63.

Ortner, Sherry B. (1984). "Theory in Anthropology Since the Sixties." *Society for Comparative Study of Society and History*. Vol. 26, No. 1 (Jan 1984). Pp. 126-166. Accessed June 20, 2013 at stable URL <http://www.jstor.org/stable/178524>.

Patton, Michael Quinn. (2002). *Qualitative Research and Evaluation Methods*. 3d ed. Thousand Oaks, CA: Sage.

Pedersen, J. (1986). Madrasa. In: C.E. Bosworth, E. van Donzel, B. Lewis and Ch. Phellat (eds) *Encyclopaedia of Islam*. New Edition. Vol. 5 KHE-MAHI. Leiden: E.J. Brill.

Pelkmans, Mathijs. (2005). *Baptized Georgian: Religious Conversion to Christianity in Autonomous Ajaria*. Max Planck Institute for Social Anthropology Working Papers, No. 71. Halle/Saale, Germany. Accessed on Feb. 9, 2014 at stable URL <http://www.jstor.org/stable/4623068>.

_____. (2007). "'Culture' as tool and an Obstacle: Missionary Encounters in Post-Soviet Kyrgyzstan. *The Journal of the Royal Anthropological Institute,* Vol. 13, No. 4 (Dec 2007), pp. 881-889. Accessed on Feb. 9, 2014 at stable URL <http://www.jstor.org/stable/4623068>.

Peters, R. (2002). "Wakf" in *The Encyclopaedia of Islam, New Edition. Vol. XI.* Ed. P.J. Bearman, et al. Leiden: Brill.

Peters, Rudolph and Gert J.T. DeVries. (1977). "Apostasy in Islam." *Die Welt des Islams, New Series*. Vol. 17, Issue 1/4, pp. 1-25

Pew Forum for Religion in Public Life. (2012). The World's Muslims: Unity in Diversity (survey report). Washington DC: Pew Research Center. Accessed on April 22, 2013 at stable URL: < http://www.pewforum.org/uploadedFiles/Topics/Religious_Affiliation/Muslim/the-worlds-muslims-full-report.pdf>.

Poliakov Sergei P. and Olcott Martha Brill. (1992). *Everyday Islam: religion and tradition in rural Central Asia*. Armonk, N.Y.: M.E. Sharpe.

Polkinghorne, D. (1988). *Narrative Knowing and the Human Sciences*. Albany: State University of New York Press.

Radford, David. (2011). *Religious Conversion and the Reconstruction of Ethnic Identity: An Investigation into the Conversion of Muslim Kyrgyz to Protestant Christianity in Kyrgyzstan, Central Asia*. Thesis submitted for the Doctor of Philosophy, Discipline of Sociology, School of Social and Policy Studies, Faculty of Social and Behavioural Sciences, Flinders University of South Australia.

Rambo, Lewis. (1982). "Current Research on Religious Conversion." *Religious Studies Review.* Vol. 8 (1982): 146–59.

_____ . (1993). *Understanding Religious Conversion New Haven, Conn.: Yale University Press.*

Rashid, Ahmed. (2002). *Jihad: The Rise of Militant Islam in Central Asia.* New York: Penguin Books.

Reidhead, Mary Ann and Van A. (2003). "From Jehovah's Witnesses to Benedictine Nun: The Roles of Experience and Context in a Double Conversion." In *The Anthropology of Religious Conversion,* ed. Andrew Buckser and Stephen D. Glazier. Oxford: Rowman & Littlefield.

Riessman, Catherine Kohler. (1993). *Narrative analysis.* Vol. 30. Sage.

Ro'i, Yaacov. (1995). *Muslim Eurasia: Conflicting Legacies.* Yaacov Ro'i ed. Portland: International Specialized Book Services.

Sanneh, Lamin. (1989). *Translating the Message: The Missionary Impact on Culture*, Maryknoll, New York: Orbis Books.

_____ . (2008). *Disciples of All Nations.* Oxford: Oxford University Press.

Sayid A. (2006). *Interview with author.* Osh , Kyrgyzstan.

Segal, Alan F. (1990). *Paul the Convert: The Apostolate and Apostasy of Saul the Pharasee.* New Haven: Yale University Press.

Silver, Brian. (1974). The Impact of Urbanization and Geographical Dispersion on the Linguistic Russification of Soviet Nationalities. In *Demography.* Vol. 11, No. 1 (Feb., 1974), pp. 89-103. Accessed Jan 1, 2011 at stable URL: <http://www.jstor.org/stable/2060701>.

_____ . (1976). Bilingualism and Maintenance of the Mother Tongue in Soviet Central Asia. *Slavic Review.* Vol. 35, No. 3 (Sept), pp. 406-424.

Sherkat, Darren E. and John Wilson. (1995). Preferences, Constraints, and Choices in Religious Markets: An Examination of Religious Switching and Apostasy. *Social Forces*, Vol. 73, No. 3 (Mar), pp. 993-1026. Accessed Nov. 1, 2010 at stable URL <http://www.jstor.org/stable/2580555>.

Shnirelman, Victor. "A Symbolic Past" in *Russian Politics and Law*, Vol 48, No, 5, Sept-Oct 2010, pp. 48-64.

Spuler, Bertold. (1972). *History of the Mongols, based on Eastern and Western Accounts of the Thirteenth and Fourteenth Centuries.* London: Hippocrene Books

Stark, Rodney. (1996). *The Rise of Chiristianity.* New York: HarperCollins.

Stark, Rodney & Rodger Finke. (2000). *Acts of Faith: Explaining the Human Side of Religion.* Berkeley: University of California Press.

Stipe, Claude E., Ethel Bolssevain, Ronald J. Burwell, Vinigi Grottanelli, Jean Buliart, Herman Hochegger, Rodolfo Larios Nunez, Lucy Mair, Martin Mluanda, William H. Newell, Martin Ottenheimer, Glenn T. Patersen, Delbert Rice, Michael A. Rynkiewich, Frank A. Salamone, Robert B. Taylor, Julio Teran-Dutari, Paul R. Turner, and Adriaan C. Van Oss. (1980). "Anthropologist Versus Missionaries: The Influence of Presuppositions [and Comments and Reply]. *Current Anthropology.* Vol. 21, No. 2 (April., 1980), pp. 165-179. Accessed on Feb. 9, 2014 at stable URL < http://www.jstor.org/stable/2741710>.

Strauss, Anselm, and Juliet Corbin. (1998). Grounded Theory Methodology. In *Strategies of Qualitative Inquiry.* Norman K. Denzin and Yvonna S. Lincoln eds. Thousand Oaks, CA: Sage

Thistlethwaithe, Susan. (1994). Settle Issues and Neglected Questions. *Journal of the American Academy of Religion.* Vol. 62, No. 4 pp. 1037-1045.

Turnbough, Jeffrey A. (2004). *A Religious Paradigm Shift for Adult Spaniards in the Conversion Process to Evangelical Christianity.* A Dissertation Presented to the Faculty of the School of Intercultural Studies. Biola University. In Partial Fulfillment of the Requirements for the Degree Doctor of Missiology.

Van der Veer, Peter. (1996). *Conversion to Modernities: The Globalization of Christianity.* London: Routledge.

Van Gennep, Arnold. (1960). *The Rites of Passage.* First Phoenix Edition; Translated by Vizdom M.B. and Caffee G.L. Chicago: University of Chicago Press.

Varisco, Daniel. (2005). *Islam Obscured: The Rhetoric of Anthropological Representation.* New York: Palgrave Macmillan.

Walls, Andrew F. (2008). "Christian Mission in a Five-Hundred Year Context" in *Mission in the 21st Century.* Andrew Walls and Cathy Ross, eds. Maryknoll NY: Orbis Books. 2008.

Warriq, Ibn. (2003). *Leaving Islam: Apostates Speak Out*: Amherst NY: Prometheus Books.

Wensinck, A.J. (1986) Kurban. In: C.E. Bosworth, E. van Donzel, B. Lewis and Ch. Phellat (eds) *Encyclopaedia of Islam.* New Edition. Vol. 5 KHEMAHI. Leiden: E.J. Brill.

Werth, Paul W. (2000). "From 'Pagan' Muslims to 'Baptized' Communists: Religious Conversion and Ethnic Particularity in Russia's Eastern Provinces. *Comparative Studies in Society and History.* Vol. 42, No. 3 (June), pp. 497-523. Accessed June 12, 2013 at stable URL: <http://www.jstor.org/stable/2696643>.

Wimbash, S. Enders. (1986). "The Soviet Borderlands" in *The Last Empire: Nationality and Soviet Future.* Ed. Robert Conquest. Stanford: Hoover Institutional Press.

Yamane, David. (2000). Narrative and Religious Expereince. In *Sociology of Religion.* Vol. 61, No. 2 (summer), pp. 171-189.

Zurayk, C.K. (1991). Djama'a. In: C.E. Bosworth, E. van Donzel, B. Lewis and Ch. Phellat (eds) *Encyclopaedia of Islam.* New Edition. Vol. 2 C-G. Leiden: E.J. Brill.

www.ingramcontent.com/pod-product-compliance
Lightning Source LLC
Chambersburg PA
CBHW081129170426
43197CB00017B/2794